KOKOPELLI

ANCIENT MYTH  MODERN ICON

BY
WAYNE GLOVER

KOKOPELLI

ANCIENT MYTH MODERN ICON

Information has been obtained from sources believed to be reliable, but its accuracy and completeness, and the opinions based thereon, are not guaranteed. Requests for additional information should be made to: Camelback/Canyonlands Publishing at 4860 North Ken Morey Drive, Bellemont, Arizona 86015, or telephone number: 520-779-3888.

Library of Congress Catalog Number: 96-084314
International Standard Book Number: 1-879924-26-9

TABLE OF CONTENTS

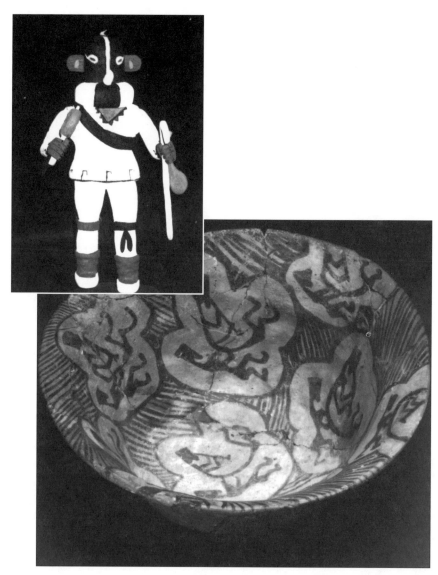

PHOTO COURTESY: JOSEPH STEVENSON COLLECTION, IN THE LAB OF ANTHROPOLOGY/MUSEUM
OF INDIAN ARTS & CULTURE, SANTA FE.

INTRODUCTION

The capricious little hump-backed image, known as Kokopelli, is a prominent fixture in the Southwest and its many gift and curio shops. He has taken the place of coyotes and cactus art in the hearts and minds of the Southwest traveler. We like him. We find him fascinatingly irresistible, whether adorning a belt, t-shirt, or handmade pottery. Thousands of items, with hundreds of variations of this petroglyph character of ancient times, seem to beckon our attention and hearts. But why?

To find the answers as to why Kokopelli appeals to us in such a way, we need to seek answers as to who Kokopelli is, and his meaning in the world today. Where did he come from? Why does he have the humped back? Is he a deity, or simply a product of lore? A mythical character created to provide amusement or to send a message? Could he have been a trickster, a seducer of maidens or the product of the story telling imagination?

While it's probably true that if you ask a hundred people what Kokopelli means, you would, in all likelihood, receive one hundred different responses; it's that unknowable element that keeps us all looking. The Kokopelli and all of his legend and lore is the absolute epitome of contradiction. The interpretations of Kokopelli are diverse and complicated in that even the Native Americans themselves are vague in their ideas and feelings concerning this character. It has been found that ideas concerning interpretations of Kokopelli differ from culture to culture, village to village, clan to clan, and even within clans.

It is further complicated when the interpretation differs from one generation to another. Adding to this confusion is an adoring and curious public, who to this point, has been unaware of the various interpretations and the importance of this image to Native Americans. Native Americans of the Southwest have had this hump-backed flute player in their cultures for a millennium.

Many Native Americans feel the intense commercialization of the Kokopelli is just one more example of their sacred images being desecrated. Others feel, however, that the popularity of the Kokopelli has increased public awareness of the spiritual and mystical values of Native Americans.

The turmoil, conflict and controversy concerning the publics' infatuation with Kokopelli and other Native American mystical images and Native Americans desire to maintain control over the images of their legends and myths has not been resolved. Preservation and education; however, may be central to resolving this issue. While this book is, in no way, an exhaustive study of Kokopelli, and while I can offer very little new on the subject, I do hope to bring together what is known in a way that will answer some questions, spark some questions and generally entertain those of you experiencing this character for the first time—or the hundredth time.

It's my hope that by communicating what is known of this character, it will spark a desire in each reader to learn more about the lives, legends, myths and religions of the many diverse Native American cultures of the American Southwest. Kokopelli is only one such myth and legend and may be a compilation of several different characters. The readers should always keep in mind that the questions concerning

Kokopelli, as well as other petroglyph characters, lie in a bed of conjecture, myth, legend, lore and unadulterated guesswork.

Petroglyphs and pictographs have provided the imagination with a kind of Rorshach test. When mixed with our cultural biases, imaginations and personal fantasies, they can develop very different meanings and interpretations. This is probably why many see the creatures depicted in rock art as space aliens, shamans or just people with deformities. Some images are part animal and part man, while other images could be one or the other.

While a number of exceptionally learned individuals have made great strides in gleaning truth from fiction; after years of painstaking research, they would probably be the first to admit that guesswork is still the paramount force in the interpretations. When seeking truth, ethnological records provide certain general interpretations when they are compared to various aspects of shamanistic symbolism, practices and beliefs. This provides most archeologists with the impetus of interpretation. Difficulties arise when the researcher(amateur or professional) forgets that numerous meanings can come from a single symbol in any given culture and can frequently occur when crossing from culture to culture.

Mythological beliefs transcend rational beliefs in that things can become much more or much less than what they were in real terms, when following a myth from culture to culture. The analogy that best interprets this is the game of gossip that most of us played in kindergarten. The game is where you whisper something in one person's ear. They in turn whisper the same thing in the next person's ear and so forth-on down the line to the end, where it usually has little, if any, of the original meaning. As generations pass on stories, fiction tends to embellish the truth. It is this researcher's belief that Kokopelli is fiction based on truth...the percentage of that truth is best left to each of us as individuals to interpret.

After analyzing several thousand pages of material, making numerous fact finding trips to the Southwest, speaking with an innumerable amount of Native Americans, librarians, researchers, academicians, museum personnel, store owners and amateur archaeologists, this researcher found that they all have an opinion. These opinions are all different, but they all believe Kokopelli's significance is great. Unlike other books and articles written on this subject, it's my belief that to answer some of the mysteries of Kokopelli, we must have at the minimum a rudimentary understanding of the world from which the Kokopelli sprang. It is for this reason that a chronology of man's history in the Americas needs to be understood. Kokopelli is a product of this history and the various cultures formed during this history.

THE BEGINNING

As the oceans solidified into the great glaciers, the land rose between what is modern day Russia and the western coast of Alaska, a span of just 48 miles. This expanse is what we now call the Bering Strait. Today, only 23 miles of open water separate the northeastern cape of Siberia from the Great Diomede Island which belongs to Russia. Another three miles of open water separate the Great Diomede Island to Little Diomede Island which belongs to the United States. It's another 22 miles from the Little Diomede Island to the western-most tip of the peninsula of Alaska. You have, by modern standards, a short boat trip. To ancient man, this trip was a formidable endeavor.

First man was curiously drawn across the Bering Strait during the Pleistocene Epoch period, or Ice Age as we commonly know it, between 30,000 and 40,000 years ago. Ice covered most of North America with one ice sheet, referred to as the Wisconsin Ice Sheet by scientists, that went as far south as present-day Iowa. Ice was said to have dropped the ocean depths by around 475 to 500 feet, creating land in areas formerly covered by water. It was one of these newly created land bridges, the Bering Strait, that first drew man from one continent to the other. Scientists have further stated that they believe the ice that covered the North American continent could have been up to one mile thick in places.

Probably intent on his hunt for game, first man never even realized that he had crossed into a new world. That game would have included saber-toothed cats, dire wolves and short faced bears, all of which are believed to have migrated from Asia, probably with man hot on the trail. Migrations of man and animal continued to occur until the end of the Ice Age about 11,000 to 15,000 years ago. As the massive ice flows started to recede North, ancient man claimed more of the south and east for his nomadic lifestyle.

Between 9500 and 9000 B.C. the North American Southwest experienced more moisture and cooler temperatures than the region does today. Mammoth, camel, horses and bison were plentiful as they grazed on the lush grasslands found in the ancient Southwest.

With the exception of a brief period around 2000 B.C. when the rains returned along with cooler temperatures, the Southwest had changed to much as it is today by around 8500 to 8000 B.C. The native horse and camel disappeared between 8,000 and 9,000 years ago, and the great mastodon last roamed North America around 6,000 years ago.

Researchers believe that by 7000 and 6500 B.C. descendants of the hunters who had first crossed the Bering Strait, now reached the southern most tip of the Americas. It has been further estimated that around 7000 to 6000 B.C. the Desert Archaic period began. It is believed by scientists that it was during this time period that four important changes took place in the Archaic (some refer to them as the Cochise) people.

The ancient hunters developed the fire drill and the grinding stone. This grinding stone is often referred to as the metate. This device was said to have been developed at the beginning of this period. Also during this period, instead of all meat diets, the use of other foods such as seeds, berries, wild grains and tubers became part of their diet.

Occurring at the time was the development and construction of semi-permanent dwellings (later in this cycle of development came the pit house), and the creation of some basic spiritual beliefs and ceremonials.

The Archaic were a foraging, hunting, nomadic people. By around 3000 B.C., most of the big game was gone, leaving small game and the need to hunt in groups. The bow and arrow was not yet available. Game was often chased and run off cliffs to make a kill. The ancient hunters also used atlatls or spear throwers. The atlatl was probably developed about 10,000 to 12,000 years ago. The bow and arrow was not developed until the time of Christ, while others believe it was between A.D. 500 and A.D. 700, that the bow and arrow was independently discovered by Native Americans in this hemisphere.

Corn is believed to have evolved from a wild grass, called Teosinte, found in many parts of Mexico. Evolution probably took the grass south into Central and South America. Some small cobs of an early variety of corn were found by researchers that were dated to approximately 5000 B.C. It was only after 3000 B.C. that corn had reached the Southwest.

Even though its presence was known, corn only reached importance around 500 B.C. when agriculture started to evolve. The burgeoning Anasazi culture had started experimenting with agriculture to supplement their hunting endeavors by around 1000 B.C. The Anasazi; however, got serious about agriculture around 500 B.C. when they were growing corn, beans and squash which had already been domesticated and traded in Mesoamerica. These items were brought northward in trade.

As agriculture took hold, so did the development of cultures, social structure and trading. The Anasazi was forming into a cultural body well in advance of their counterparts, the Hohokam and Mogollon.

The Hohokam culture may have started as early as 300 B.C. and the Mogollon may have started as early as 200 B.C. While a number of cultures were starting to form at this time, it was the three cultures of the Hohokam, Mogollon, and Anasazi that appeared to be the most dominant influences in the Southwest. While it would be inappropriate in this writing to try and compete with the volumes of material that have been written about these various cultures, they will be discussed in a limited overview in order to facilitate a better understanding as to who the Kokopelli was/is and why he came to be important to the Native Americans and to us as a modern society.

PHOTOS COURTESY PALMS TRADING
COMPANY ALBUQUERQUE, NM

ANASAZI

It's believed that the first Anasazi migrated into the four corners region around 3000 B.C. Originally, the Anasazi, along with the other primary cultures of the Hohokam and Mogollon, maintained small, widely dispersed family or clan groups who were mostly hunters and foragers. This started to change between 1500 B.C. and A.D. 500 to the establishment of a more sedentary village life. Of the three cultural groups, the Anasazi appeared to have held on to the nomadic lifestyle longer than their counterparts. While the Hohokam and the Mogollon appeared to have been influenced very early on by their neighbors to the south in the Mesoamerican region, the Anasazi, by virtue of geography, were slow to obtain some of the products and knowledge of their counterparts. It did appear, however, that once the trading of products and knowledge began after A.D. 500, the Anasazi were rapid in their pace to becoming a well-entrenched agricultural society.

The Anasazi people were short and stocky, with the men averaging about 5 feet 4 inches tall and the women averaging around 5 feet tall. Skeletal remains have been found that lead one to believe that, while not very common, some of the Anasazi reached a height of 6 feet.

For the Anasazi to live into their 40s was considered to be old age. However, some evidence exists that at least some of the people may have made it into their 70s or 80s. It's believed that this is certainly the exception and not the rule.

The Anasazi were said to have been plagued with a number of maladies that must have caused a life of pain and discomfort.

Many of the Anasazi would live for years in pain from the loss of teeth from the grit that came from the food that was ground, such as corn and nuts, on the metate. Teeth, often worn to the gums, would become abscessed. These abscesses often progressed deep into their jawbones. It's also believed that their diet, which consisted of a lot of corn with little meat, was a diet high in carbohydrates and low in protein, which could have lead to malnutrition especially in the children. It's also believed that they suffered from osteoporosis, iron deficiency anemia and respiratory problems due to the smoke from their fires and their close living conditions. The living conditions would have also promoted parasitic problems such as lice or pinworms. Broken bones were seldom set properly. Arthritis was like a plague among the Anasazi. Winters were a time of dread and death for the Anasazi; especially for the young and old of the villages. It has been calculated that up to one-third of the children died before the age of five.

Being a resourceful culture, the Anasazi adapted to the harsh environment of the Southwest. They wore clothing made mostly of hides stitched together, with strips of hide or the more common fibers of the yucca leaf, with yucca tips serving as the needle. The yucca was well utilized by the Anasazi. The wild yucca provided a banana-like fruit that they would eat. The roots were used to make a soap and the yucca fibers were used in everything from making paint brushes to sandals and baskets.

While the Anasazi grew and ate corn, beans, squash, and seeds; a study of the fecal remains of the Anasazi has shown scientists that they also ate mice, rabbit and other small fur bearing creatures, often with the fur or hair still on them. Scientists also found that the Anasazi ate cactus, again without removing all of the thorns. It's not known why they didn't eat fish, reptiles or amphibians (frogs and turtles) even though they were around. It's been speculated that they didn't eat these things due to spiritual beliefs.

Originally, the Anasazi lived in pit houses that had roofs made of brush. Unfortunately, most of these roofs were only 6 feet above the fires with which they used to cook and heat. As the archeologists reviewed the remains, they found that many of the ancient Anasazi's living quarters, as well as the Anasazi themselves, had been burned. Charred remains, since it is well preserved, have been an aid to the archeologist using radio carbon date testing or the dendrochronologist.

Around A.D. 400 to A.D. 600, the art of pottery making was introduced to the Anasazi, probably by the Mogollon people. The first attempts at pottery making by the Anasazi left a lot to be desired. They would form the pottery around a basket, then burn the basket away. They then began using the basket as a form to start the bottom of the pottery, then remove the basket. Little is known as to why they used this method of pottery making. Their pottery making improved as experimentation continued.

It was around this time that the Anasazi felt the calling to not only be creative, but to be prolific in their rock drawings. The Anasazi certainly had a broad canvas from which to draw. Their territory stretched from an area east of the Rio Grande, to what is modern day Nevada to the west of the central parts of what is modern day New Mexico and Arizona to the south and north into modern day Utah and Colorado. Their domain contained more square miles than the state of California.

The Anasazi moved into the area known as Mesa Verde around the time of Christ, but lived on the mesa top in pit houses. Around A.D. 700, they started living above ground in rooms built behind their old pit houses which now became kivas. Kivas were specific areas set aside for society meetings and worship. It was also during this transitional period that they developed the practice of strapping their babies to a hard board that traditionally has been deemed a cradle board. This practice of putting the baby on the cradle board caused the back of the infants head to be flat.

It took several hundred years for the Anasazi to move into the canyons and into their now famous cliff dwellings. It is estimated that this move took place around A.D. 1200. It seems that the Anasazi only lived in these dwellings for about one hundred years. The Mesa Verde area was abandoned by A.D. 1300.

A prolonged period of little or no rain caused soil erosion in the already overworked soils, creating a situation that was unparalleled even for the hardy Anasazi. As hard times tightened its grip on the Anasazi, they migrated south and west into what is now the land of the Hopi and the Zuni, and south and east into the Rio Grande valley area where it's believed that some Anasazi maintained communities with distinct cultural identities until around A.D. 1500. Feeling that their gods had abandoned them; the starving, disillusioned and bewildered Anasazi started the process of abandonment of not only Mesa Verde, but of Chaco Canyon and numerous other Anasazi communities.

The Anasazi will forever be known for their architectural endeavors, as the Mogollon are known for their pottery and artistic processes, and the Hohokam for their water management systems.

During the Anasazi zenith, they constructed multi-family dwellings unequaled in size and magnitude in the United States until the 1870s. Despite not having the wheel or beast of burden, they constructed hundreds of miles of roads, with many 20 to 30 feet in width. Theories abound as to why, but no one knows for sure why such an elaborate system of roads was built. The Anasazi created some of the finest pottery of the ancient cultures. They also developed unique systems of security for their communities, as well as a very active trading system with their neighbors.

The droughts brought a scarcity of food that turned Anasazi against Anasazi and broke the cycle of peace they had known. It seemed that when the greatness finally collapsed, it did so with an uncommon swiftness.

It has been estimated that tens of thousands of Anasazi sites still await discovery in the Southwest. Archaeologists have located more than 25,000 Anasazi sites in New Mexico, with at least that many discovered in Arizona. Add to this the thousands more found in Utah and Colorado, and you have an idea of the vastness of this once sturdy and influential nation.

LEFT: PHOTO COURTESY
OF MAXWELL MUSEUM
OF ANTHROPOLOGY,
UNIVERSITY OF NEW
MEXICO, ALBUQUERQUE

HOHOKAM

In an area that roughly covers 45,000 miles in the Sonoran Desert of modern day Arizona, lived a culture of people who have been referred to as the Hohokam. Hohokam (Ho-ho-KAM) arguably started as a culture around 300 B.C. from hunters and gatherers who had occupied the surrounding mountains and deserts for several millennium. Early researchers believed that the Hohokam were migrants from Mesoamerica and not inhabitants of the region. As with most of the information about the early cultures, the opinions expressed by the early researchers, as well as current researchers, are open to controversy and speculation.

The Hohokam built their homes mostly out of a soil found in the area called caliche. Caliche, when mixed with water and allowed to dry, made a rock hard surface similar to our modern day cement. The Hohokam's early homes were much like the early homes of the other cultures, which were round pit houses. They later built a more rectangular style pit house.

Unlike their neighbors, the Anasazi, the Hohokams claim to fame was not their architecture but something far more important to them in the environment they chose to call home. The Hohokam were a creative and diligent people who had, for the most part, successfully designed, built and maintained a sophisticated irrigation system in the middle of the Sonoran Desert. The system was made up of diverse dams, headgates and canals. Like their neighbors, they didn't have the luxury of the wheel or the beast of burden. They only had stone tools, digging sticks and baskets to haul out the debris. Despite these handicaps, they built over 300 miles of major canals, and over 1,000 miles of small feeder canals.

While it's not known for sure where they acquired this knowledge, it is a good assumption that the basic knowledge probably came from their neighbors in Mesoamerica and was supplemented with a great deal of good old trial and error. Most researchers believe that the Hohokam started the irrigation systems sometime around A.D. 500.

By A.D. 600 to 700 the Hohokam were growing cotton, corn, beans, barley and domesticated agave. Somewhat later, their agricultural endeavors added tepary and lima beans along with tobacco, pumpkins, squash, and amaranth. Along with the items they grew, they ate prickly pear cactus pads and fruits, cholla cactus buds, saguaro fruits and the protein rich beans from the mesquite tree. They would normally grind the mesquite beans into a flour.

From an artistic standpoint, the Hohokam were best known for their shell crafts such as beads, bracelets and pendants. They carried their ability to work with shells to the point where they had learned to do fine etching on the shells with an acid made from fermented saguaro cactus juice. They harvested the shells from the beaches of the Gulf of California, then transported them about 200 miles back to their homeland. The products they made from the shells were highly desirable trade items that have been found in the ruins of their neighboring cultures. They also traded in obsidian for the materials to make lance heads, arrows and knives, hides, salt, feathers, pottery, copper bells and rubber. Even though their pottery never reached the artistry of the Anasazi or Mogollon (Mimbres), it did contain some interesting designs and characters—with one very distinct piece that contained dancing Kokopelli and Kokopellimana that was found in Snaketown, Arizona (see photograph page 4).

While there's little question that they were masters of desert survival, there are many more questions about other aspects of their lives, such as why were they the only one of the major cultures and one of only a few of all the cultures to practice cremation of their dead. They also appeared to have a class system of have and have-nots. They had, and used, what appears to archaeologists as ball courts. The early Hohokam ball game played on these courts was probably an early form of Poc-Ta-Poc, a Mesoamerican sport used for recreation, gambling, ritual, or a combination of all three. The ball courts started showing up around A.D. 700 to 800 and appeared to have disappeared around A.D. 1200.

While the irrigation systems provided several hundred years of existence for the Hohokam, it also provided copious amounts of frustration with silt build-up and battles with salt that came about from water evaporating in the hot desert sun. The ever present struggle against drought and flooding has been speculated as the downfall of the Hohokam. By the mid 1300s, the Salt and Gila Rivers started experiencing massive flooding that washed out canals and holding dams. It has been surmised that this protracted battle with the elements was the beginning of the end for the culture known as the Hohokam. According to researchers, the Hohokam probably ceased to exist as a distinct culture at some point around A.D. 1400.

MOGOLLON

The Mogollon (MUGGY-own) maintained a homeland that was said to have been larger than that held by the Hohokam and Anasazi combined. Their lands ranged from grassy valleys, to forested mountains to deserts so inhospitable that the main materials with which to build and maintain a residence were yucca and creosote bushes. It's believed by many that the Mogollon culture grew out of the Cochise people who were occupants of the Southwest six thousand years before the time of Christ. The Mogollon formed into a distinct culture around 200 B.C.

Mogollon people sustained an existence as hunters much longer than their neighbors, the Hohokam and Anasazi. Like their neighbors, they started out living in pit houses, later progressing to rectangular pit houses, then adopting above ground multi-roomed pueblo styled structures like the Anasazi.

While the Mogollon embraced some of the water management systems of the Hohokam, they never came close to the progress made by the Hohokam. The Mogollon seemed to value a shared community lifestyle. It is widely believed that the Mogollon were the first to learn pottery making, then in turn, they shared this knowledge with their neighbors. Their manufacture of black-on-white pottery seemed to have been a reciprocal trade with the Anasazi, but the artwork, especially of the Mogollon peoples, called the Mimbres, declared a strong similarity to art found on pottery produced by the Hohokam.

25

Most of their crops were grown in high valleys where the growing seasons were limited and required constant watch and maintenance. They grew corn, squash, kidney beans, and later cotton and amaranth. Their diets also consisted of pinion nuts, walnuts, acorns, prickly pear cactus pads and fruits, sun flower seeds and various meats obtained through their vigorous hunting activities.

The Mogollon people who lived in the Mimbres Valley have been referred to by scientists as the Mimbres people. The Mimbres people created pottery of artistic excellence from around A.D. 100 to 1150. Their artwork has told a great deal about their culture, and in a sense, of their downfall as a culture. The designs ran, from expressing the mundane, to the whimsical and mystical. It was common for the Mimbres to place a bowl over the head of a deceased person with a "kill hole" punched in the bottom to presumably allow the person's spirit, or possibly the vessel's spirit to escape to the afterworld.

Even though the Mimbres and Mogollon, in general, were prosperous and eating well, environmental changes were starting to unravel the confidence and strength of this culture. It's been interpreted from their art that by the 1300s their political and social systems were starting to disintegrate.

By the 1400s, the Mogollon had melted away and combined with other cultures. Many believe that the Mogollon and the Anasazi combined to form the Western Pueblo culture. The Western Pueblo culture probably became the Hopi and Zuni peoples. It's also been speculated that the Mogollon, or a part of the Mogollon people, melted into the Mexican Indian culture called the Tarahumara.

	HOHOKAM	MOGOLLON	PUEBLO	
PRESENT			PUEBLO V	PRESENT
1700				1700
1600			PUEBLO IV	1600
1500				1500
1400				1400
1300	CLASSIC	MOGOLLON IV	PUEBLO III	1300
1200				1200
1100				1100
1000	SEDENTARY	MOGOLLON III	PUEBLO II	1000
900				900
800			PUEBLO I	800
700	COLONIAL	MOGOLLON II		700
600			BASKET-MAKER II	600
500				500
400				400
300	PIONEER	MOGOLLON I	BASKET-MAKER I	300
200				200
100				100
A.D.				A.D.
B.C.				B.C.
100				100
200				200
300				300
	FORAGERS	FORAGERS	FORAGERS	
7000				7000
	HUNTERS	HUNTERS	HUNTERS	
10000				10000

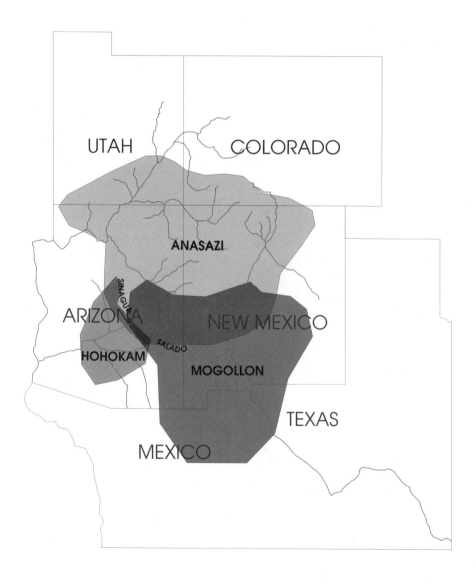

EXPLORERS TO PIONEERS

On August 3, 1492, the Spanish sovereigns, Ferdinand and Isabella, sent forward with their blessings a 41 year-old seaman by the name of Christopher Columbus to find a new route to the Indies. Christopher Columbus was christened in Genoa in 1451 with the name of Christoforo Columbo. Christopher Columbus is the Latinized version. His name meant "Christ Bearer."

On October 12, 1492, at approximately 2:00 a.m., a lookout on one of the caravels sighted an island in the Bahamas that Columbus promptly named San Salvador. Since Columbus thought he was in the Indies, he called the natives he encountered, Indians. His exploration opened the flood gates to other adventurers and explorers, who roared through the New World with a vengeance.

This world would eventually be called America due to Amerigo Vespucci. Vespucci was an Italian navigator who visited this hemisphere in 1499 and went back to write accounts of what he saw. In 1507, Martin Waldseemuller, a German geographer who had read some of Vespucci's writings, decided to call the new world America on the maps he was drawing.

After more than 700 years of conflict and battle with the North African Moors, Spain arrived in the 15th century as probably the most powerful and influential nation in Europe. With this new found power, Spain felt it's destiny to conquer the world in the name of the

Spanish Crown and the Catholic Church. They perceived their mission in life was to spread the light of God to the godless, as well as to seek wealth. It has been estimated that 200,000 Spaniards crossed the Atlantic to find a future in the New World.

It was with those righteous goals of spreading Christianity and obtaining wealth that Hernando Cortes subdued the great Aztec empire and Francisco Pizarro conquered the noble Incas. In just one generation, the Spaniards acquired more new territory than the Roman empire conquered in five centuries.

A Spaniard by the name of Alvar Nunez Cabeza de Vaca told fascinating stories that he had heard from the Indians about hunchbacked cows (which we know as buffalo) and more importantly, about cities with streets paved with gold. They were called the "Seven Cities of Cibola."

In 1539, the Viceroy of Mexico, Antonio de Mendoza, sent Fray Marcos de Niza, along with a black man named Esteban (also spelled Estevan and known as Estavanico and Stephan), a Moorish slave, to seek out these cities of Cibola. It was Esteban who failed to fare so well on this trip. He was killed for insulting the village elders in the reported city of Cibola by asking for turquoise and women. Some stories say he was shot full of arrows, while other stories say he was killed and cut into pieces. Others say he was stoned to death. It's also these story variations that say he was killed for seducing the women of the village. It's for that reason that some have given credence to the legends that Esteban was the original Kokopelli.

The theory certainly holds some intrigue but has problems in its timing, since Kokopelli very much pre-dates Esteban. Esteban was killed at the village of Hawikuh (Cibola, according to the Spanish). Hawikuh village now lies in ruins close to the New Mexico village of Ojo Caliente on the Zuni Indian Reservation. Fray Marcos, for fear of the same fate as Esteban, never entered the city on this trip. He did, however, return to Mexico in one piece to tell of what he saw and heard, still believing that riches were there to take.

On April 22, 1540, Francisco Vazques de Coronado led Mexican Viceroy Antonio de Mendoza's most famous expedition into the Southwest. Coronado's band of followers consisted of 300 Spaniards, approximately 1,000 Indians and over 1,500 horses, mules sheep and cattle. At least four friars accompanied Coronado, with Marcos de Niza at the helm. When Coronado marched into what is modern day New Mexico in 1540, it was estimated that there were 85 pueblos. Today, only 19 pueblos survive.

With time, the conquest of the Southwest brought Spanish officials to seize farmlands, exact tribute and to spread their religions while attacking the religions of the pueblo peoples. The Spanish Franciscan padres, in their zeal and haste to convert the Indians to the Christian religions, caused the destruction of shrines, altars and representations of the old deities. They led the natives to forget many of what the padres deemed as pagan gods, ceremonials and symbols. In 1610, the first Spanish settlement of Santa Fe was founded.

By 1680, the Pueblo Indians had had enough of Spanish domination. Under the secret leadership of a San Juan Pueblo medicine man named Pope', they rose up against their oppressors in a revolt. In August of 1680, the Pueblo people fought back against the Spanish, killing priests and administrators. In the process, they destroyed missions and overtook Santa Fe. The 1680 revolt gave the Pueblo people a short-lived twelve year freedom. Diego de Vargas regained control of Santa Fe in 1692 without firing a shot or one casualty. While the Spanish introduced iron tools, the horse, cattle and Christianity, they also brought measles, smallpox, cholera and syphilis to the Indian.

In 1821, Mexico declared its independence from Spain. The peace of the Southwest was somewhat short-lived. After only 25 years, war between Mexico and the United States broke out. The U.S. won the war in 1848, but border disputes smoldered on until 1853, when the border, as we know it, was defined and established with the Gadsden Purchase.

Meanwhile, other things were occurring in the Southwest that would shape things for all time. The Santa Fe trail was established in 1821 by William Becknell. This trail poured people and goods into this area until the Santa Fe railroad took over the duties in 1880. New Mexico became a state on January 5, 1912 making it the 47th state of the United States. Arizona entered the union on February 14, 1912 to become the 48th state.

It has been estimated that at the onset of the exploration of America one and one-half million Native Americans inhabited this country. By the late 1800s, only 250,000 still survived. The settling of the Southwest was tumultuous at best and cost many lives. The Native Americas saw the loss of their freedom and way of life. Even today, over 450 years after Coronado's introduction to the Southwest, the Native Americans of this region are desperately seeking to maintain a hold on their customs, ceremonials and religions.

While history of the Southwest, like other parts of the country, could fill volumes, I've tried to provide a very cursory look at this region. Not to rehash information that most of us received in school, but again to provide a setting in which the legend of Kokopelli was born and has been nurtured during his existence.

Kokopelli is one of the more recurring figures in Southwest art.
PHOTO COURTESY: JOSEPH STEVENSON COLLECTION, IN THE LAB OF ANTHROPOLOGY/MUSEUM
OF INDIAN ARTS & CULTURE, SANTA FE.

ROCK ART

Kokopelli is but one symbol found in rock art. Rock art can be found in every state in the United States including Alaska and Hawaii. Rock art extends north to south from Alaska to the southern tip of South America. The highest concentration is; however, in the southwestern part of the United States. While rock art was undoubtedly observed by the Spanish explorers in the Southwest, they made little mention of them in their journals. One exception was at what is now called Painted Rock State Park in Arizona, which is close to Gila Bend, Arizona. Early Spanish explorers made note of the rock carving of the area, calling them "Piedras Pintadas" or painted rocks. The first notes made about rock art were made by English settlers in Massachusetts, and later by Father Marquette in his explorations.

There are basically two types of rock art, petroglyphs which are rock engravings, and pictographs, which are rock paintings. Petroglyphs tend to be the most common type in North America. Petroglyphs are drawings on stone done by pecking, incising, scratching, drilling or any combination of these techniques. They are most often done on sandstone, volcanic basalt or granite, especially in the Southwest. Pictographs tend to be found in caves and overhangs, or in other protected areas. Petroglyphs are often found together with pictographs. Rock art has been described as hieroglyphs, picture writing, ideographs, iconographs and rock graphics.

There are probably as many reasons for rock art as there is rock art. Some of the reasons could be clan symbols, astronomy, the recording of an event or a series of events, expression of a vision seen by the artist, a prayer site for one or more individuals, puberty and/or fertility rites, aimless scribbling, and the most suspected reason of all, is shamanism. (Sha'man and medicine man are one and the same in most Native American cultures.)

Shamans, considered individuals of great power, were said to have the ability to mentally transport themselves through various levels of consciousness to communicate with the supernatural by means of trances, dreams, visions and fasting. Shamans possessed inborn sensitivities, a sacred knowledge of healing and the ability to communicate with the spirit world. Their ability to travel beyond ordinary and traditional boundaries by altered state of awareness could allow them to see the future and travel not only great distances, but inward for knowledge of the human body and mind. Horns worn as a headdress were almost always emblematic of shamanistic and supernatural powers. Birds may also symbolize the shamans power and the magic of flight.

Native American rock art is a type of archaeological remains. With the variety and distribution area of rock art its study and interpretation is of particular importance in understanding the lives and religions of the Native American peoples.

Even with this importance, until recently, rock art study has maintained a low priority with most professional archeologists. It has been estimated that serious rock art study has only taken place in the last 30 to 35 years. The reasons for its low priority have probably been the difficulty in dating rock art, assigning it to a specific group or culture, relating to known cultural sequences and interpreting the art in a scientifically acceptable way. Basically, the task of interpreting rock art is complex and difficult, causing much of what has been interpreted to fall in the realm of conjecture and guesswork.

Somewhere during the research on this project, I remember reading that the study of rock art, for the most part, had been carried on by unqualified amateurs, or pseudoscientific researchers who have provided extravagant hypotheses, questionable interpretation, and countless unsupported conclusions. This may be true, but as art in general should stir controversy, then so should the interpretation of rock art. It was the unqualified amateur that kept the spark alive before the professional archeologist raised the priority level to a point that qualified rock art as worthy of their attention.

While we could all be caught up in the controversies surrounding interpretation, the issue of our rock art being devoured in the name of progress holds a much higher priority. In the process of building roads, dams, water projects and the construction of homes and businesses, we are destroying for all time thousands of petroglyph sites.

In the early processes of working petroglyph sites, archaeologists were reluctant to disclose site locations for fear of having them vandalized. Then there was a shift to the thinking, that with a greater public awareness and understanding of the significance and fragility of rock art, people would be less likely to destroy it. The thought was expressed by one researcher that chalk, print and rifle bullets have taken their toll on the Southwest canvas. While vandalism is still a problem in many areas of the Southwest, education has shown some signs of saving our venerable heritage.

While it was believed that preservation and education would become the corner stones in the survival process of rock art, one element was left out of that realm of thinking. As expanding highway systems started making once inaccessible archaeological sites more accessible, the risk increased dramatically for both intentional and unintentional damage and vandalism. At one museum, while doing research, I was told of an elderly couple who were caught sawing a petroglyph out with a masonry saw. When they were arrested, they just couldn't understand what they were doing wrong.

Recent newspaper articles have conveyed a reversal of the earlier position held by archaeologists in that sites should be off limits to the general public. This new effort to hide locations has risen from a growing concern of both federal authorities and researchers in recent years about looting. People are loving the ruins and rock art to death.

It's not just man who is the villain in all of this, it is nature itself. Unlike our modern art galleries where art can be roped off or enclosed in glass, rock art is vulnerable to the natural wear and tear of wind, rain and moisture. Many sites have been destroyed by flooding, natural erosion and fire. We need to find a balance that allows us to view and appreciate the ruins and art before they succumb to the elements.

It has been said by some that rock art is like poetry on stone, while others see signs of ancient astrology, signs of diabolic cults, or possibly even markers for buried treasure. The rock tells a story, but we must be willing to listen. It's very obvious that rock art, and in particular the Kokopelli, has caught our attention, and thus our quest for more information, on the subject.

KOKOPELLI

As I explore the ages in my quest for meaning in Kokopelli, I find that I've advanced into a realm of hypothesis and speculation a universe of mystery, magic, shamans and creatures in the likeness of man, but possessing mystical callings.

Kokopelli is a reflection of cultures long gone and cultures now dealing with change and the ever present encroachment of modern ways. The Indians of the Southwest tenaciously hold on to the religious beliefs that echo those of their ancestors. It's balance that has affected, to some degree, every aspect of the Southwest Native Americans lives. The Native Americans of the Southwest see themselves as being inextricably woven into the natural scheme of the entire universe. They are men with the joys, cares, worries and problems of man, but they also are the sands, winds, stars, thunder, lightning, rain, sun, moon and seasons. They are these and all of the other things that are born, live, and die in the cycle of existence. Kokopelli, for whatever his reasons, is a thread in that fabric of life.

Researchers believe that the earliest flute playing figures came from the Anasazi Basket Maker III period which was between 400 and 700 A.D. The early depictions were of stick figures who were often shown seated, often alone, but sometimes in pairs.

This flute playing figure is one of the few rock art symbols that have survived in a basic recognizable form from the early days of the Anasazi into modern times. While it's believed Kokopelli appeared in his early stages during the Anasazi Basket Maker III period, the exact date of his creation is unknown. What is known is that he appeared with the humped-back and flute in Anasazi rock art, and pottery decorations after 1,000 A.D., with frequency. It's never been clear if the early images of the flute players were to depict real people or mythical images.

ATTRIBUTES OF KOKOPELLI

As with the overall image of Kokopelli, his attributes also contain contradiction and controversy. The first images of what has been commonly known as Kokopelli contained the material attribute of a flute or flute like protrusion, but none of the other attributes associated with Kokopelli, namely the humped-back or the phallus.

While rock art, even with natural erosion and man-made vandalism, has proven to be a very durable form of communication, it is not a very precise form of communication. As images were pecked into the stone, detail in the image was not conducive to the medium. While most would look at the images of Kokopelli and assume that the long protrusion in front of his face is a flute, it could in reality, be any one of a number of other things.

It's been theorized that this protrusion could be a style of whistle, a prayer stick, smoking device or some other item used in ceremonies. It has also been intimated by numerous researchers that the protrusion is a snout. They cite that the Hopi people alone have several Kachinas (supernatural beings) that have beaks, snouts or other protrusions, that if their likeness was pecked into rock with the same lack of detail as early rock art, the similarities to Kokopelli could be close.

The flute, as we will assume is the appendage protruding from Kokopelli's face, goes back to the time of Christ in the American Southwest. Among the Hopi people, it is used both ceremonially and for everyday musical purposes and is considered a very sacred item.

41

But it was also important to their ancestors, the Anasazi. The Anasazi used rattles made from wood as well as deer hoofs. They also made flutes from wood and from bone, normally bird wing bones. These instruments were used to accompany their ceremonies and possibly for day to day entertainment and communication. Numerous flutes have been found in burial areas indicating the importance of the flute to the Anasazi people. It can only be assumed that this same importance for the flute would carry over to the person who had the ability to make music from the flute. This person must have been held in high regard by his people. Could this be how the Kokopelli started?

The flute and flute music are held in high regard by the Hopi, Zuni and the other Pueblo people of the Southwest. It appears that the original hump-backed flute player legends originated in the village of the upper Rio Grande area of what is now modern day New Mexico and with time were filtered into the Hopi and Zuni peoples at the villages of Walpi (Wal'PEE) and Sichomoui (Si'-Co'-MO-VEE) on First Mesa, probably by the Asa (Tewa) Clan.

While this is generally believed to be the path taken by this legend, other theories do hold some merit. It has been suggested that Kokopelli is an ancestor of the Callahuayo Indians of the Andes in South America. They were known to travel from village to village with their wares and play their flutes to announce their arrival and to let people know that they were friendly.

Even in modern times, the Quichua Indians of Chochabamba continue to play the flute and carry a pack on their backs while traveling through the Andean Highlands.

It could be that the original concept of Kokopelli came from the Anasazi by contact with traders from South America, or the more common Mesamerican traders called Pochteca, who travel from village to village trading their wares. The Pochteca have been known to play a flute to announce their arrival, and they also had a reputation in the traveling salesman game of being womanizers. It's believed that the Pochteca arrived in the Southwest around A.D. 1060 and may have started out as Toltec or Aztec people. They worked from an area in the Mexican state of Chihuahua (as it is known now), called Casa Grandes. Timing of the Pochteca and the proliferation of petroglyph drawings of Kokopelli creates some interesting possibilities.

Among the Yuma Indians (commonly called Yuman Indians), the flute is used by the young men during the process of courting, but is seldom, if ever, used during group ceremonies.

With the Hopi people, Kokopelli is identified with the hump-backed flute player when he borrows a flute from Lenang, the flute kachina during the Hopi-mixed kachina dances.

In the Hopi culture, Kokopelli serves more as an intermediary between man and the gods. He is a kachina who is associated with fertility of not only man, but animals and crops, and is a mythological cousin to the Hopi's other fertility figures.

At Zuni, he is equated with Ololowishkya, (a fertility figure who dances in the plaza during winter ceremonies) Chu'Lu'Laneh (a fertility figure and the name of the flute he plays) or Paiyatyamu (the Zuni deity of flowers, butterflies and music). Paiyatyamu uses a flute, and in Zuni legends, his magical butterflies along with his music result in methods of seduction. All three deities have to do with fertility to some degree.

This relates somewhat to the Hopi cultural belief that the flute is a summertime instrument played to promote flowers and growth. Again, the constant subject of fertility and propagation continues to permeate the cultures of the southwestern Native Americans. It is interesting to note that Kokopelli is notably absent in accounts of the flute ceremonies of most of the Pueblos and the Hopi.

Many researchers have expressed over the years a belief that Kokopelli was never a person but an insect, possibly a locust or dragon fly. Some evidence tends to lend value to these theories. It is legend that the locusts play the flute to melt the snow when appealed to by the sun-loving snakes. Locusts also are the musical and curing patrons of the Hopi flute societies. Locusts play a key role in the Hopi legends of their emergence from the inner worlds. During this emergence, the locust played his flute and guided the Hopi people to the earth's surface from the inner worlds as lightening continued to strike him.

There is at least one other area where the flute could be something other than a flute. The appendage could be a smoking device. Among the Pueblo Indians, smoking is a formal process to begin and end ceremonies. It's said that smoke clouds carry individual prayers to the sky, then blend with the clouds to bring rain, which is the lifeblood of the Pueblos. For most of the Pueblo cultures, smoke symbolizes clouds.

As a recap of the reasons for the use of flute in the realm of southwestern Native American cultures, the most noted are: to win the love of a maiden, to compete with one another, to encourage rain and the flowers of spring, to announce their presence as visitors or traveling traders as they enter a village, and to draw the curious mountain sheep into bow and arrow range.

Kokopelli is a compilation of a number of attributes. While each has significance, collectively they become Kokopelli. While the flute is apparent in modern renditions, it's only part of the modern Kokopelli. The arched or humped-back provides a sense of him dancing. When combined with the flute, the commercial appeal is heightened.

Bent or arched figures are found in a number of Anasazi wall paintings. It's not known if these figures were based on images of themselves, as many were bent or humped over due to injuries and arthritis, or a character drawn from the mind based on a real or imagined character. From an ethnomedical standpoint, it's believed that prehistoric bone, joint and spinal tuberculosis may have existed with some frequency in the cultures of the Southwest. Humps have been associated with supernatural powers. What is not known is why or how that belief of association began.

Traditionally, items have been worn, held and carried on the backs of Native Americans since the beginning of time. It's also common to see items carried on the backs of kachinas and other mythological personages. While most items carried on the back are for mundane reasons and day-to-day chores, it's not unusual to see items carried by individuals for ceremonial purposes.

While a number of kachinas either play flutes or have phallic appendages, few kachinas are hump-backed. Many, however, wear items on their backs that create a protrusion which gives the impression of a hump such as an arrow quiver, a basket, a burden bundle, other person or an animal (see photograph front cover).

Even someone with a bent over or hunched posture or pose, could be identified as having a hump. In the realm of rock art, a gift filled

45

pack, a burden basket carried for mundane purposes or any other back protrusion could be conceptualized into a hump-back. It's also unclear whether the hump-back is hollow or solid.

Some kachinas are hunched over to simulate animals on all fours as in deer dances. There are also several bent or hunch-backed kachinas that simulate old age. Like the appendage of a flute or flute like snout, the hump can have a lot of contradiction and controversy attached to it.

Even the legends concerning the hump and its contents are varied. At Hano, the Hopi Tewa village, it's believed that Kokopelli's hump is filled with buckskin for making shirts and moccasins which are traded for brides. In the Tewa speaking Pueblo of San Ildefonso, the Kokopelli legend is that he is a wanderer who goes from village to village with a bag of songs on his back, trading new songs for old. My favorite is Ghaan'ask'idii, the Navajo hump-backed deity who is said to have in his feathered hump, mist and seeds for all types of plants. According to some versions, his hump is made of a rainbow, while others believe that the hump is filled with mist, seeds and rainbows.

Yet another interesting version is that a Mayan deity called Ek Chuah is an ancestor of Kokopelli. Ek chuah wore a pack on his back that looked like the hump on the Kokopelli. Ek Chuah is said to be the patron god of bee keepers, hunters, traveling merchants and cacao growers.

In the modern images of Kokopelli, his ever present flute and his arched dancing body are immediately recognizable attributes by most who have frequented the American Southwest.

Earlier images of Kokopelli also contained the attribute of an erect phallus.

As I tread into this area of Kokopelli's attributes, I find a twinge of embarrassment, not at the subject matter, but at my inner conflicts concerning my beliefs as a person of Native American heritage and an individual with a stilted puritanical upbringing. Unfortunately, it's that same sense of Puritanism that has robbed some of our Native American cultures of a part of their identities.

Native Americans were a people whose sole existence rested on nature and her bounties. Exhibitions of sexuality were not meant to be displays of vulgarity, obscenity or perversion. They were demonstrations of an important and deeply meaningful part of their natural existence. It was only when the Spanish Missionaries came in and told the Native Americans that their displays were obscene, that they became obscene.

The great American author and humorist, Mark Twain, wrote or made two quotes which I believe hold value at this point:

Nature knows no indecencies; man invents them.
MARK TWAIN *(Notebook, 1935)*

Man is the only animal that blushes. Or needs to.
MARK TWAIN
Pudd'nhead Wilson's new calendar.
Follow the equator (1897) 1.27.

The major forces in all southwestern Native American cultures, were the need for water and the growth and reproduction of food sources and people. Keeping these basic tenets and ideological concepts in mind, it's not surprising that the phallus, as a fertility symbol, showed up so frequently in ancient rock drawings and as a prominent attribute of Kokopelli.

All throughout the Southwest, both male and female figures with exaggerated genitalia have been found in rock drawings, as well as the ceremonials of the various Native American cultures. After all the idea of human, animal and vegetable propagation were/are primary concepts in religion, ceremonials and art of almost all of the ancient and modern southwestern Native American cultures.

Kokopelli as the ancient myth, and Kokopelli as the modern icon has been almost always associated with fertility and seduction. Propagation and its related symbolism is not exclusive to Kokopelli or his sister spirit Kokopell'Mana. At Acoma and Zuni, several kachinas display the phallus or demonstrate sexual or erotic moves as part of their dances and displays.

In the Navajo culture, there is a deity called be'Yotcidi, which means One-Who-Grabs-Breasts, who has allegedly had intercourse with everything. The early performances of these, and other characters, were labeled by observers who happened to be white and very prudish, and the government as lewd, obscene, and notoriously obnoxious. It was primarily the Hopi kachina dance that got the most attention. In the Hopi culture, it was said that on occasion, Kokopelli would come to the plazas where he would try to entice young girls with things that he holds up for them to snatch, but somehow he never seems to catch them.

To other Hopi, Kokopelli is an individual who comes with a burden basket of babies on his back which he leaves with the young married women. Kokopelli's "sister spirit" kachina is Kokopell'Mana who comes to the villages in the springtime. The Kokopell'Mana (which is portrayed by a man) is thought to be crazy about men and will chase them at great speed (usually played by the fastest runner). If she catches one, she flings him to the ground and imitates the sex act to the delight and roars of laughter of the crowd. If the man escapes, he is rewarded with corn, the paper thin piki bread or some other delicacy.

When discussing the phallic symbolism and the Kokopelli, keep in mind the theories discussed early in this book about the medical aspects of his attributes, extend to this attribute as well. Some researchers believe that the ithyphallic (erect phallus) is the result of a condition called priapism which is permanent or semi-permanent engorgement of the penis, a possible symptom in the ancient cases of tuberculosis which was believed to have been present in the Southwest.

The word priapism comes from the name Priapus, which in both Greek and Roman mythology was a fertility god. He was the offspring of Aphrodite and Dionysus.

Whether the phallus shown on early depictions of Kokopelli was added by the unconscious idle doodling of an artist, or a symbol drawn to indicate fertility, or the interpretation of an individual with a physical malady, it has certainly added mystery and, of course, more contradictions as an attribute of Kokopelli.

PUEBLO/NAVAJO BELIEFS

Kokopelli's identity transcends attributes and suppositions about those attributes. He has cultural identity, albeit as diverse in interpretation as his attributes. As cultural differences are shown, it should again be kept in mind that Kokopelli and his existence is a shared commodity by most all of the Southwest cultures.

Similarities exist in the interpretation of Kokopelli, as in other aspects of religion and cultural identifiers, because of the sharing of information over the last 1,000 years between cultural groups. This sharing occurred through trading, sharing of villages during adverse times, ceremonial gatherings and other intermingling of cultures.

Ideas, beliefs and legends were shared and picked up by another culture to provide an answer for something that was lacking, a viable explanation in the course of existence. What is to be attempted now is to provide you with an overview of some of the key groups in the Southwest, who they are, and how they view Kokopelli.

PUEBLO

A common bond among all Pueblo Indians is that religion transcends and permeates all that is their life and in essence is the core of their life. Their arts, crafts, industries, social structure and religion is interwoven into the fabric of existence and this is what

50

creates the bond that is the Pueblo Indians of the Southwest. As with all of their non-Pueblo neighbors in the Southwest, food, shelter and general survival is what motivates everything. It is through their beliefs and religion that all is given significance. They maintain individual governments from each other and they are geographically different. They don't believe in marriage outside of their own communities.

As the Spanish explorers filtered through the Pueblo region in the 1540s they found flutes and flute playing very prominent in the ceremonies of the Pueblo people. It's been surmised by numerous researchers that the Pueblo people used flutes to signal between themselves and as a general communications device for security of their villages.

Many of the Pueblo Indians believe that the flute players depicted in rock drawings were done while groups of their people migrated from one area to another. The Hopi say that Kokopelli never played the flute although this is widely debated among the Hopi and their other Pueblo neighbors.

On First Mesa is the village of Hano (ha'-no) which means "Eastern People" when derived from the word "Anopi". Hano could also be a derivation of Tanos which was the Spanish name for the Tewas. The Tewas that occupy Hano came from the upper Rio Grande country of present day New Mexico. The Tewa ancestors were probably Anasazi whose hunger drove them from the four corners area to Posi, which was close to the modern day community of Ojo Caliente. According to researchers, Posi was abandoned by the Anasazi around A.D. 1500 and split up to become the six Tewa Pueblos of San Juan, Santa Clara, San Ildefonso, Tesuque, Pojoaque and Nambe'.

The Tewa of Hano have a legend about Kokopelli that describes him as a large black man called Nepokwai-i or Nipokwaiye. They claim this kachina comes with a big sack on his back filled with buckskins and other materials to make shirts and moccasins for the young women of the village. Others indicate that Nepokwai-i could be kin to or the same as Panwu, the mountain sheep kachina.

If you have ever seen Acoma, it is not hard to understand why it's referred to as Sky City. Acoma is about 65 miles west of present day Albuquerque, New Mexico. Acoma sits on a 365-foot sandstone mesa. It's believed that Acoma was established on or near its present location around 900 A.D. and has been continuously occupied since 1075 A.D., creating their claim of being the oldest continually inhabited community in the United States. The Hopi village of Oraibi also makes this claim. Acoma (AH-Koh-Mah) was believed to be made of Chaco culture Anasazi. The Acoma people use the Keres (Kay-rays) dialect for their native language. From a dialectic standpoint they share a bond with the Laguna Pueblo people. Both are considered to be western Keres, and share a somewhat distinct linguistic difference from that of the eastern Keres.

The most familiar story of Kokopelli in the Acoma society is the one concerning the Dapopo brothers (Kokopelli) and their seduction of the war chief's daughter.

The Dapopo Brothers Seduce the War Chief's Daughter[2]

A long time ago two Dapopo brothers lived at Acoma near the house of Masewi, the elder of the twin war gods. (For a description of the Dapopo brothers, consult Leslie White, The Acoma Indians Forty-seventh

Annual Report, Bureau of American Ethnology, 1932, p.77). The younger Dapopo asked the War Chief's daughter to let him sleep with her, but she refused. In fact, the chief's daughter rejected the advances of all the boys at Acoma.

The Dapopos were angry and kept thinking of how they could get the girl. At last the older brother advised the younger to dig a hole in the ground at the side of the mesa and hide there until the girl came to relieve herself in the evening. In this way the Dapopo got his girl. She did not realize exactly what had happened, but she liked the sensation so much that she repeatedly returned to the same spot. The older brother hid there and he, as well, got the girl. Soon the Acoma people noticed that she was going to have a baby. Everyone wondered about it because "she never did have a man," and every boy tried to claim that he was the father of her child. When the time came two babies were born, one for each of the Dapopo. The War Chief decided to find out who had fathered his daughter's children so he announced a test. This test would involve all the young men and boys of the village. They gathered bunches of flowers. Then they had to line up and offer them to the babies. If a baby accepted the flowers they would pass the test. All the other men tried, but the babies would not accept them.

Finally the Dapopos, who were last in line, presented their flowers and the children took them, thus acknowledging the Dapopos for their fathers. All the other men and boys felt ashamed and angry. They called the Dapopos "Big Ears" because they had enormous ears, and they talked against the chief's daughter for having let them father her babies. The Dapopo brothers brought some things for the children to wear and went to the girl's house to live.

For a more complete description of the Dapopo brothers in the legend of Acoma, it is suggested that you consult the work of Leslie A White, The Acoma Indians (47th Annual Report, *Bureau of American Ethnology*, 1932), p.77.

The Acoma people have another kachina that holds some similarities to Kokopelli, called Naiyu. Naiyu are kachinas who look up women's dresses during ceremonies, giving the women sexual desires.

HOPI

The Hopi (hoe-PEE) name is a contraction of Hopituh which translates to "The Peaceful Ones." Hopi legend tells that before the earth was created, the spirits lived in a world called Tokpela, which to them means a boundless space. After much wickedness, their first world was destroyed by fire. Their second world was destroyed by ice. The third world was characterized by chaos. It was the fourth world (the present one) that the people emerged to stability.

The Hopi are considered to be the undisputed experts at dry farming. With a growing season of approximately 135 days and an annual rainfall of about 10 to 12 inches a year, they would have to be. Because of the natural forces surrounding their lives, their beliefs in the powers of the supernatural forces became very important to them. The Hopi are considered to be the most intensely religious culture in the Southwest. The Hopi people leave little doubt about their cultural diversity. They are a culture comprised of numerous clans that have had several cultural ties with both ancient and modern Southwestern peoples.

In past times, when the Hopi people would experience a severe drought, they would move in with their Zuni neighbors, thus sharing many of each others cultural beliefs and customs. It is probably for this reason that the Hopi and Zuni people are culturally the closest of the Southwestern Native American cultures.

During the Spanish occupation of the Southwest, they were one of the few Pueblos that resisted the Spanish Missionaries to the degree that they did. They maintain more of their religious beliefs than most of the other Pueblos. Today, they are known by both tourists and serious collectors as the premiere craftsmen in silversmithing, carved kachinas, baskets, pottery and weavings.

The Hopi occupy a reservation of about three million acres where they have 12 villages on three mesas. Their reservation is surrounded by the 17 million plus acre Navajo reservation. The Navajo and Hopi have a number of sacred and significant sights in their corner of the world, but one of the most important is the San Francisco peaks that are located north of present day Flagstaff, Arizona. The Hopi people believe that the entire surface of the San Francisco peaks is sacred and the home of their kachinas. They believe that this is the spot where their kachinas rehearse and prepare themselves for the making of clouds to produce rain and snow for their lands. They believe that the kachinas manifest themselves as clouds over the peaks.

This deeply religious belief comes from centuries of viewing this for themselves and has therefore become an unshakable force in the Hopi view of the world. To many Native American cultures, mountains are sacred because they are the birthplace of clouds.

A major preoccupation with the Hopi and other Southwestern cultures is rain. It is said that the Hopi can raise corn and other crops on as little as eight to ten inches of rain a year, allowing them to maintain an existence where other farmers would have given up. It is from their need of rain and the propagation of men, animals and crops that one could surmise is the reason that so many of their kachinas have to do with rain, animals, insects and fertility. Many of these deities have to do with at least the support of these important endeavors. The Hopi believe that Kokopelli is an influential force in fertility and abundance, whether it be in the hunt, the fields, or in human reproduction.

Hopi translation is difficult concerning Kokopelli because it's not clear whether they are discussing a flute player or a fly. Among the Hopi, Kokopelli has been referred to as the Assassin or Grey Desert Robber Fly (Promachus Vertebratus) kachina; but when he borrows a flute and plays it during a dance, he is referred to as the hump-backed flute player. To other Hopi, Kokopelli is an individual who visits with other kachinas with a burden of babies on his back, which he leaves with the young married women of the village. He is also considered to be an intermediary between men and the gods.

Another interpretation is that Kokopelli is a rain priest who calls the clouds and moisture with his flute. Kokopelli has also been associated with insects such as the locust. Locust is the musical and curing patron of the Blue and Drab Flute Societies of the Hopi. This has probably manifested itself from the Hopi Emergence Myth where the locust was sent to look for an entrance into the upper world. As he emerged, the clouds shot lightning bolts through him, but he continued on his way, and continued to play his flute. (In a different version of this story the locust was shot and died, but came back to life). It's also said that locusts play their flutes to melt the snow when appealed to by the sun-loving snakes.

Another insect that is often related to the Kokopelli stories is the dragonfly, because of his hump-back look and because he is a persistent copulator. According to the Hopi, Kokopelli is the symbolic figure of the Asa Clan which came from the upper Rio Grande country of present day New Mexico. He has also been linked in representation to the Spider Clan, Water Clan and the Titmouse Clan.

Of all of the Southwest cultures, the Kokopelli seems to be the deepest rooted in the Hopi culture. While his meaning varies from culture to culture and village to village, the basis of his existence still dictates that he is key to the fertility of crops, animals and man. He's a communicator and link between man and the gods. His connection with rain alone makes him a force of exceptional prowess to the peoples of the Southwest.

The legends of kokopelli extol a simple message of survival for the indigenous people of the Southwest. Kokopelli, in his many roles as rain priest, flutist, hunter, warrior, minstrel, god, insect and lecher, comes across as an unprincipled amoral force that holds a duel role, that at the same time can bring order and security to a chaotic world.

The Hopi existence and religious view does not seek to harness the mysteries of life or to control those mysteries, but it is their belief to acknowledge, honor and preserve them. Kokopelli is ancient wisdom, a spiritual helper, who comes as a simple spiritual manifestation that is neither good or bad as is man. Kokopelli, like man, is just one strand in the spiritual web of life.

Occasionally, Kokopelli comes to the plazas where he tries to entice
the young girls with things that he holds up for them to snatch, but
somehow he never seems to catch them. He has a "sister" kachina,
Kokopell'Mana, who comes to the villages in the springtime. This "girl"
kachina (portrayed by a man) is thought to be crazy about men and
will chase them at great speed. If she catches one, she flings him to the
ground and imitates the sex act to roars of laughter from the village
audience. If the man escapes, he is rewarded with piki bread, corn or
some other delicacy.

The Story of Kokopele[2]

At the time when Oraibi was first inhabited, the katcina Kokopele
was living nearby with his grandmother. (She was neither named
nor identified by the story's informant.) Within the village there dwelt
a good-looking girl who was so vain (qwivi) that she rejected the
advances of all the young men to make her acquaintance. (A common
motive in Hopi mythology concerns girls who are too vain or too "fussy"
to follow normal patterns of sexual behavior. Such girls generally have
adventures with supernatural creatures, as in the case of the present
myth). At last Kokopele confided to his grandmother that he meant to
try his luck with this pretty girl, but his grandmother laughed at him
because he was hump-backed and far homelier than many of the
Oraibi boys. Nevertheless, the katcina insisted that he was going to
make an attempt to win the girl.

Now Kokopele had noticed that every noon, soon after lunch, the girl
was in the habit of going to a particular spot at the edge of the mesa to
perform her natural functions. (At the old village or Oraibi, on top of

Third Mesa, people conceal themselves as best they can at the edges of the mesa. No privies of any kind are used, and no particular section is set aside for the use of either sex).

It was by taking advantage of her regular procedure that Kokopele meant to win his mistress. His first step was to dig a trench leading from his house to the exact spot which the girl was accustomed to visit. Then he cut and hollowed out a number of reeds, fashioned them into a continuous pipe, and laid it in the ditch. This done, he filled in the trench and smoothed it over so that the girl would notice nothing wrong when she came to her accustomed place.

Soon after noon the next day, the girl came to the spot she generally frequented for such purposes and bent down to perform her office. Hardly had she finished than she felt something stirring under her, and enjoying the sensation, made no effort to investigate. It was the penis of Kokopele that she felt, for so cleverly had he arranged his hollow tube that on inserting his organ into it at home he was enabled, thanks to its unusual length, to direct it into the girl's vagina. (The unusual length of the penis is one of the distinctive characteristic of Kokopeltiyo. Hopi Journal of Alexander M. Stephen, Columbia University Contributions to Anthropology, Vol. 23, 1936, p. 388).

From then on Kokopele never failed to take advantage of his device nor did the girl abandon her customary visits to this spot. At last she found herself pregnant, but neither she nor any of the people in the village had the slightest idea of her lover's identity. Try as they might, neither angry relatives nor jealous rivals ever succeeded in getting a glimpse of the girl's sweetheart, and when in due time a boy was born to her, his paternity was as much a mystery as ever.

That spring, one of the men in the village announced a foot race of a special kind. To the young men and boys he made a speech saying, "We all know that an unmarried girl has had a baby here lately and we would like to know the man who is responsible. Let every one go out and pick a bunch of pretty flowers for himself. Then we will race while the girl sits here nursing her son and as each man finishes let him hold out his bouquet and the baby will grasp the one that is held by his father."

As the girl was still very much desired by many of the young men, each was eager to win the race in order to be the first to stretch forth the flowers in the hope that the baby would grasp them. When Kokopele heard the news he was afraid that he might lose his mistress, so he told his grandmother that he meant to compete with the others. Again she discouraged him, saying, "I don't think that the child will like you because you don't look very pretty. I'm afraid you won't come out lucky."

Nevertheless the katcina persisted, and went out with the young men of Oraibi to pick a bouquet. The next day, however, poor Kokopele found himself entirely unable to cope with the other runners and he was still far from the finish when the winning racer arrived at the village and hurried to offer his flowers to the baby. Much to his chagrin, he made no impression on the little boy, nor did the other men fare any better when they had finished. At last the badly tired Kokopele, far behind all the other runners, succeeded in reaching his goal. Hardly had he stretched forth his bouquet than the child grasped it eagerly. All were dumb founded, but the race sponsor kept his word.

"Now my girl," he said, "We have found out who is the father of your son and that is what we wanted to know. Now take this katcina to your home and keep him for your husband."

This the girl was only too glad to do, and she lived happily with Kokopele who, being a katcina, was a good provider and helped his fellow villagers by bringing lots of rain. And yet, despite his kindness, he somehow aroused the jealousy of the Kwitavi (Feces Kiva) group who plotted to take his wife away from him. One evening they invited him to come to their kiva to spin yarn, but among themselves it was understood that they would conceal weapons in the kiva and beat him to death. (Stories of kiva jealousy and attacks similar to that on Kokopele are repeated with numerous variations in several Hopi myths. Compare H.R. Voth, The Traditions of Hopi, Anthropological Series, Field Columbian Museum, Vol. 8, 1905, pp. 126-35. In other stories told at Oraibi, the term Kwitavi "Feces Kiva" is often used).

However, the Katcina got wind of the plot and consulted his grandmother, who told him that the men were jealous of his pretty wife and advised him to seek help from the Spider Woman. When he had sought her out, Spider Woman promised her aid. "You are hump-backed katcina," she said, "but I will give you a good medicine. When the Kwitavi chief asks you to spin in his kiva do not be afraid to go there. Then, when it comes time to rest and eat, they will put out the fire and try to kill you. Just as soon as it gets dark, chew your medicine and spurt it everywhere. This will make all the men hump-backed like yourself, and when they try to find you by your hump they will be fooled into beating each other. Just you jump up and hang to the rafters and you will be safe."

The next day everything happened just as the Spider Woman had foretold. The men spun yarn from dark to midnight and then gathered about for the feast that was to be their reward. Hardly had they begun to eat, then the kiva chief extinguished the fire and plunged the kiva into total darkness. Immediately Kokopele chewed and spurted his medicine and got a safe hold on the rafters while the wicked men, feeling each other's humps, began to belabor one another as hard as they could. At last they realized that there seemed to be many humpbacks present, so they called for lights and discovered that some of their own kiva mates had been killed or injured but that Kokopele was entirely unharmed.

The men from Kwitavi were witches and "two-hearted," so they soon recovered their natural shapes, and were healed of their wounds or restored to life as the case might be. Even then their wickedness did not go unpunished, for within a few days they all died off one after the other.

Alarmed by his narrow escape from death, Kokopele decided to leave Oraibi and to live with his family at the home of his grandmother just outside the village limits. Here things prospered well with him and within a few years enough children were born to him to enable him to stage a dance for his former neighbors.

"Reproduced by permission of the American Anthropological Association from American Anthropologist 41, 1939. Not for further reproduction."

ZUNI

Zuni (Zoo'-Nee) is the name said to be the Spanish version of the Keresan name of Sunyi. The Zuni call themselves A'shiwi which means "the flesh." Others, however, say the translation means the "flesh of the flesh." It is said that linguistically, Zuni is unrelated to any other tribe in the Southwest. Zuni is the largest pueblo in New Mexico and the Zuni people are more culturally akin to the Hopi than any other Pueblo. Zuni is one of 19 Indian pueblos in modern day New Mexico that covers an area from Taos to Albuquerque.

Each of the pueblos, like Zuni, are independently governed and all maintain a unique identity from the others. The Zuni believe that their ancestors emerged from beneath the earth and wandered for many years until they settled on Hacona Itwana, which means middle ant hill of the world.

It was the Zuni pueblo at Hawikuh that Fray Marcos believed was the first of the famed seven cities of Cibola. After the death of Esteban at this pueblo in 1539, Fray Marcos returned to Mexico and led Coronado, the first of many Spanish invaders to this country. Between the Spanish occupation, and in later years, the raids of neighboring Apaches, the pueblo of Hawikuh was abandoned in 1672. The Zuni, like the Hopi, resisted the Christianizing efforts of the Spanish clergy and were able to maintain much of their religious beliefs and heritage. It's been widely believed that the Zuni culture is made up of Anasazi from the Chaco Canyon area and the people of the Mogollon culture.

An old Zuni myth tells about the abandonment of the Anasazi cliff dwellings. This myth says that a giant, called Cloud Swallower devoured men and consumed "the cloud-breaths of the gods, and souls of the dead, whence descends rain....snow ceased in the North and West; rain ceased in the South and the East, the mists of the mountains above were drunk up; the waters of the valley below were dried up...."

Other supernaturals, namely the twin gods of war and Grandmother Spider, destroyed the dreadswallower of clouds. "But fearing that never again would the waters freshen their canyon, our ancients who dwelt in the cliffs fled away to the southward and eastward...all save those who had perished aforetime; they are dead in their homes in the cliff towns dried, like their cornstalks that dried when the rain stopped long ago, when all things were new." The author of this myth is unknown, but the myth adds credibility to the belief that the Zuni was made up at least partially from the disillusioned Anasazi of Chaco Canyon.

The Zuni say that Kokopelli is an immensely successful rain priest, with the ability to make it rain at will. The Zuni also say that he has been pictured on the rocks around their country for the purpose of attracting clouds and moisture to the area. They sometimes refer to him as Chu'Lu'Laneh, which is the name for the type of flutes used by their rain priests. There exists in Zuni mythology a flute playing cultural hero called Paiyatamu. He is not hump-backed. However, he plays a flute, and like the Hopi, Kokopelli is associated with fertility. Phallic images without flutes are often referred to as "Ololowishkya." The Ololowishkya dances during the winter ceremonies and is also a fertility figure.

Another story that has circulated in the Zuni and Acoma cultures, and may have first come from the Navajo of Chaco Canyon, tells of an old legend of Kokopelli. The legend says that a gambler, who won all of the Zuni peoples possessions, was afflicted with disease after the Zuni people appealed to other deities for help and the deities took pity on the Zuni people. The gambler was accompanied by a flute player who perished with the gambler when he died.

NAVAJO

avajo (Na-Vah-Ho) is the name that comes from the Tewa (TAY wah) peoples word Navahuu which means, depending upon who you talk to, "the arroyo with the cultivated fields" or "the enemies of the cultivated fields." The Tewa most often referred to the Navajo as Apaches de Nabahu, which may account for the variation in the definition. The word, Navajo, has also been spelled Navaho. The modern tribal government prefers the Navajo spelling. The Navajo people; however, refer to themselves as the Dine', which again has several different definitions, such as tribe, nation or the preferred "the people."

Most of the North American Athabascan (or Athapaskan) Indians originally lived in what we now identify as the state of Alaska and in the northwestern provinces of Canada. It is believed the Athabascans followed the eastern foothills of the Rocky Mountains to the southern part of Colorado where part of the group moved to the southwestern part of Kansas, the Oklahoma panhandle and the Texas panhandle to become the Kiowa-Apache. Some settled into northwestern New Mexico to become the Navajo. Others divided up to become various factions of the Apache. Most of this migration occurred in the late 1400s to around 1500. It is believed that some earlier groups or small bands came into the area earlier. Little was written or known of the Navajo until the 1600s.

In 1680, during the Pueblo Revolt, a number of Pueblo people sought refuge with the Navajo. It was during this time that the Navajo, a simple culture, was greatly influenced by its contact with the Pueblo cultures. It was the Pueblo who taught them to work a land in an environment that would require constant adaptations and adjustments. The Navajo adopted many of their guests customs, religious ceremonies and art forms including rock art and sand paintings.

The Navajo land occupation started out in the north and northwest part of current day New Mexico. In the late 1700s, the Navajo people started expanding westward. It was also in the 1700s, that the Navajo acquired the horse and then proceeded to wreak havoc on the Spanish and later the Anglo settlers. From the 1860s to the 1880s, the Navajo's had moved far enough west and south to start crowding the Hopis. In 1962, the federal court system got involved in the land disputes which still continue to this day.

The Navajo moved into and claimed lands which had been Anasazi centuries before. As they moved into this land the Navajo became aware of the many ruins and petroglyphs located throughout the area. It was probably a natural sequence for them to add their new and old cultural beliefs to the perpendicular world of canyons and cliffs in the form of rock art.

The Navajo also have a humped-back deity or (Yei) god they call Ganaskidi, who possesses some characteristics of the mountain sheep. It's believed that this image is in at least supernatural control over the mountain sheep. It's believed that the hump on the back of Ganaskidis is made of clouds containing seed for all types of vegetation. He's also often described as a god of harvest, plenty and moisture. Some say his hump is made of rainbows, while others feel that the hump is filled with rainbows. The Navajo deity carries a staff which could also indicate that he is a guardian of sheep. The horns he wears on his head could signify, as in a number of Native American cultures, that he has been given supernatural powers.

While this deity was introduced to the Southwest after the Anasazi images of Kokopelli, he is in a sense, the Navajo equivalent of Kokopelli with parallels to the Pueblo versions.

POCHTECA

One of the more common theories regarding the ubiquitous Kokopelli is that he represents a Pochteca, an Aztec or Toltec trader, from central Mexico. In a pack on his back, he brought copper bells, pyrite mirrors and the feathers of macaws and other tropical birds to trade with the Pueblo people for turquoise and other items of value. Just as the Mexican Pochteca are depicted, he carried a flute to announce his arrival, so that people would not take him for an enemy.

Deities and legends that parallel Kokopelli can be found in the cultures of Panama, Costa Rica, Nicaragua, Guatemala, Mexico and Peru. It's believed that many parallels exist between the Aztec rain god cult of Tlaloc and the Pueblo kachina cults. Many of the Aztec deities are interestingly equated in Pueblo kachinas.

The link between Kokopelli and Mesoamerica seems to be more than a minor occurrence. As was mentioned earlier in this book, the timing of the Pochteca traders and the proliferation of the Kokopelli in rock art is compelling in its coincidental schedule.

CONCLUSION

The anomaly known as the North American Southwest is far more than mountains, deserts, cactus and Indians. The region is a unique blend of reality and illusion, of nature, the natural and the supernatural. This is a region steeped in myths, mysteries and ancient meanings. The Kokopelli and his many counterparts play but a minor part in this vast landscape and its history; but without question, a minor part that has endured through the centuries.

Kokopelli is the symbolic form of a character that seems to be created of a seemingly infinite number of manifestations. Many researchers caution that the name Kokopelli should be used more as a catch-word to describe a group of characteristics than to a single image.

Until recently, most information on Kokopelli suggested that he was not a particularly outstanding character in the pueblo pantheon. Certainly the most positive aspect of Kokopelli is that his popularity and his image has created interest in other Native American images and myths. Kokopelli gives us a chance at a conduit to another reality. Kokopelli, at the rudimentary level, is but a drop in the pool of ancient wisdom. Kokopelli, while more mystery than solution, has more than most of the Southwest images, piqued our curiosity and tantalized our imaginations. We should follow the lead of the Native American religions which does not seek to harness or control them, but to strive to acknowledge, honor and preserve them.

As you have found in this book, legends have branded Kokopelli as a priest, kachina, warrior, shaman, lecher, trader, hunter and god. He could be all of these—or none. He could have been a real person or merely the product of the imagination.

Whatever the reasons for his creation around a thousand years ago, his current popularity seems to flourish in the good feelings he produces with his dancing and flute playing image.

Some would say that his commercial use desecrates a Native American image. Others believe his use promotes awareness of Native American cultures and religions.

As a writer, artist, Southwest merchant and person of Native American descent, I see and understand both sides of the equation. It's my belief that Kokopelli, while only a minuscule portion of the infinite sea of spirituality of the Native Americans of the Southwest, should be viewed by all as a sacred piece of history and of cultures who still live in the world in which we share.

There is no question that his presence has created interest in and promoted awareness of the Southwest and its many diverse cultures.

Native Americans believe in balance. It's when we get out of balance that undesirable things occur.

Learn about Kokopelli and his thousands of spirit helpers. Protect our links to the past and learn from them. Rock art is an odyssey into time that requires our attention. Kokopelli is only one design in rock art. It is also only one piece of the puzzle that makes up the history of the Native American Southwest.

NOTES

1. The story of the Dapopo Brothers is based on a myth
    recorded by Dr. White at Acoma in 1927. This story is
    reprinted with permission from *American Anthropologist*,
    (M.S., 41, 1939)

2. *The Story of Kokopele*, by Mischa Titiev, reprinted with
    permission.from *American Anthropologist*

APPENDIX 1:
BIBLIOGRAPHY AND SELECTIVE READINGS

Alpert, Joyce M., *Kokopelli—A New Look at the Humpback Fluteplayer in Anasazi Art.* American Indian Art Magazine Winter 1991.

Arnold, David L., *Pueblo Pottery— 2,000 Years of Artistry.* National Geographic, Vol. 162, No. 5, pp. 593-606, 1982.

Bahti, Tom, *Southwestern Indian Tribes*, KC Publications, Las Vegas, Nevada, 1968.

Beaty, J.J., *The Petroglyph Puzzle.* Pacific Discovery Vol. XVI, No. 3, (May—June) 1963.

Beck, Warren A. and Ynez D. Haase, *Historical Atlas of the American West*, University of Oklahoma Press, Norman, Oklahoma, 1989.

Bolton, Herbert E., *Coronado—Knight of Pueblos and Plain*, The University of New Mexico Press, Albuquerque, New Mexico, 1949.

Brill, Lois, *"Kokopelli: An Analysis of his Alleged Attributes and Suggestions Toward Alternative Identifications"*, (Masters Thesis in Art History, UNM), 1984.

Brody, J.J., *Mimbres Painted Pottery*, University of New Mexico Press, Albuquerque, New Mexico, 1977.

Browning, Tim, "Spirits in Stone." *National Parks*,
Vol. 63, pp. 37-39, 1989.

Bush, Bamey, *Petroglyphs*, Greenfield Review Press, Greenfield
Center, New York, 1982.

Canby, Thomas Y., "The Anasazi—Riddles in The Ruins."
National Geographic, Vol. 162, No. 5, pp. 554-592, 1982.

Castetter, Edward F., "Early Tobacco Utilization and Cultivation in
The American Southwest." *American Anthropologist*,
Vol. XLV, 3, 1943.

Cordell, Linda S., "Late Anasazi Farming and Hunting Strategies:
One Example of a Problem in Congruence."
American Antiquity, Vol. XLII, No.3, pp. 449-61, 1977.

Creamer, Winifred and Jonathan Haas, "Search for the Ancient
Ones—Pueblo." *National Geographic*, Vol. 180,
No. 4, pp. 84 99, 1991.

Crosby, Harry, "Baja's Murals of Mystery." *National Geographic*,
Vol. 158, No. 5, pp. 692-702, 1980.

Cushing, Frank H., "Origin Myth From Oraibi." *Journal of
American Folklore*, Vol. XXXVI, pp. 163-170, 1923.

Cutler, H.E., "Medicine Men and the Preservation of a
Relic Gene in Maize." *Journal of Heredity*,
Vol. XXXV, pp. 290-294, 1944.

Dutton, Bertha P., *American Indians of The Southwest*
University of New Mexico Press, Albuquerque, New
Mexico, 1983.

Ezell, Paul H., "Is There a Hohokam-Pima Culture Continuum?" *American Antiquity*, Vol. XXIX, pp. 61-66, 1963.

Ferguson, William M. and Arthur H. Rohn, *Anasazi Ruins of the Southwest in Color*, University of New Mexico Press, Albuquerque, New Mexico, 1987.

Fewkes, J. Walker, "Hopi Katcinas." *Twenty-First Annual Report*, *Bureau of American Ethnology*, Washington, D.C., pp. 3-126, 1903.

Fewkes, J. Walker, *"The Cliff Ruins in Fewkes Canyon."* Mesa Verde National Park, Colorado, Holmes Anniversary Volume, pp. 96-117, 1916.

Gladwin, Harold S., *A History of the Ancients Southwest*, Bond Wheelwright, Portland, 1957.

Grant, Campbell, *Rock Art of the American Indian*, Thomas Crowell, Co., New York, New York 1967.

Grant, Campbell, *Canyon de Chelly—It's People and Rock Art*, University of Arizona Press, Tucson, Arizona, 1978.

Griffin-Pierce, Trudy, "Navajo Ceremonial Sandpaintings: Sacred, Living Entities." *American Indian Art Magazine*, Vol. 17, pp. 58-67, Winter 1991.

Gumerman, George J. and S. Alan Skinner, "Synthesis of the Pre History of The Central Lilltel Colorado Valley, Arizona." *American Antiquity*, Vol. XXXIII, No. 2, pp. 185-199, 1968.

Hadlock, Harry L., "Ganaskidi—The Navajo Humpback Deity of The Largo." (Essay), *Archeological Society Press*, Albuquerque, New Mexico, pp. 179-210, 1980.

Haines, F., *How the Indian Got the Horse*, American Heritage,
New York, New York, 1964.

Hammack, Lauren C., "Effigy Vessels in The Prehistoric American
Southwest." *Arizona Highways*. pp. 33-35, February 1974.

Haley, Florence, "Kokopelli of The Prehistoric Southwestern Pueblo
Pantheon." *American Anthropologist*, Vol. 39, pp. 644-647, 1937.

Heizer, Robert Fleming, *Prehistoric Rock Art of California*,
Ballena Press, Ramona, California, 1973.

Hill, Beth, *Indian Petroglyphs of The Pacific Northwest*, Hancock
House Publications, Saanichton, B.C., 1974.

Hofer, Hans, *Native America*, Houghton Mifflin Company,
Boston, Massachusetts, 1993.

Kidder, A.V., and S.J. Guernsey, "Archaeological Explorations in
Northern Arizona." *Bureau of American Ethnology Bulletin
No. 65*, (Washington, D.C., Government Printing Office), 1919.

Kirkland, Forrest, *The Rock Art of Texas Indians,* University of
Texas Press, Austin, Texas, 1967.

Kluckhohn, Clyde, and Dorothea Leighton, *The Navajo*, Harvard
University Press, Cambridge, Massachusetts, 1974.

Lambert, Marjorie F., "A Rare Stone Humpbacked Figurine From
Pecos Pueblo, New Mexico." *El Palacio*, Vol. 64, pp. 93-107, 1957.

Lambert, Marjorie F., "A Kokopelli Effigy Pitcher From
Northwestern New Mexico." *American Antiquity*, Vol. 32,
pp. 398-401, 1967.

Lessard, F. Dennis, "Plains Pictographic Art: A Source of Ethnographic Information." *American Indian Art Magazine*, Vol. 17, pp. 62-69, 1992.

Linne, S., "Humpbacks in Ancient America." *Ethnos* Vol. 4, pp. 161-185, 1943.

Mallery, Garrick, "Pictographs of the North American Indian." *In Fourth Annual Report of the Bureau of American Ethnology*, (Washington, D.C.: Government Printing Office), 1886.

Mallery, Garrick, "Picture Writing of the American Indians." *In Tenth Annual Report of The Bureau of American Ethology,* (Washington, D.C.: Government Printing Office), 1893.

Marshack, Alexander, "Exploring The Mind of Ice Age Man." National Geographic Vol. 147, pp. 64-89, 1975.

Matson, Richard Ghia, "Basketmaker II Subsistence: Carbon Isotopes and Other Dietary Indicators From Cedar Mesa, Utah." *American Antiquity,* Vol. 56, pp. 141-459, 1991.

Mays, Buddy, *Ancient Cities of the Southwest*, Chronicle Books, San Francisco, California, 1982. "Guide to Indian Ruins (In the American Southwest)." *Historic Preservation*, Vol. 37, pp. 50-54, February, 1985.

McKern, Will Carleton, "Western Colorado Petroglyphs." *Colorado State Office, Bureau of Land Management*, Denver, Colorado, 1978.

McMann, Jean, *Riddler of The Stone Age: Rock Carvings of Ancient Europe*, Thames and Hudson, New York, New York, 1980.

Miller, Jay, "Kokopelli." (Abstract), *Department of Anthropology—University of Washington*, Seattle, Washington, pp. 371-380, 1975.

Minnis, Paul E., "Prehistoric Diet in The Northern Southwest: Macroplant Remains from Four Corners Feces." *American Antiquity*, Vol. 54, pp. 543-563, July, 1989.

National Geographic, *The World of The American Indian*, National Geographic Society, Washington, D.C., 1974.

Neary, John, "Kokopelli Kitsch." *Archaeology,* Vol. 45, p. 76, August 1992.

"Historic Messages." *Archaeology,* Vol. 45, pp. 62-67, Nov./Dec. 1992.

O'Neill, Brian, "Kansas Rock Art." *Historic Preservation Department—Kansas State Historical Society*, 1981.

Ortiz, Alfonso, "Through Tewa Eyes—Origins." *National Geographic*, Vol. 180, No. 4, pp. 6-13, 1991.

Ortiz, Alfonso, *The Tewa World: Space, Time and Becoming in a Pueblo Society*, University of Chicago Press, Chicago, Illinois, 1969.

Packard, Gar, and Maggy Packard, *Suns and Serpents: The Symbolism of Indian Rock Art*, Packard Publications, Santa Fe, New Mexico, 1974.

Page, Jake, "Inside The Sacred Hopi Homeland." *National Geographic*, Vol. 162, No. 5, pp. 607-629, 1982.

Parsons, Elsie Clews, "The Social Organizations of the Tewa of New Mexico." (Memoirs) *American Anthropological Association,* No. 36, 1929.

Parsons, Elsie Clews, "The Humpbacked Flute Player of the Southwest." *American Anthropologist*, Vol. 40, pp. 337-338, 1938.

Reichard, Gladys A., *Navajo Medicine Man Sandpaintings*, Dover Publications, New York, New York, 1977.

Renaud, Etienne B., "Kokopelli: A Study in Pueblo Mythology." *Southwestern Lore*, Vol. 14, pp. 25-40, 1948.

Sando, Joe S., *Pueblo Nations: Eight Centuries of Pueblo Indian History*, Clearlight, Santa Fe, New Mexico, 1992.

Schaafsma, Polly, *Indian Rock Art of the Southwest*, School of American Research, Santa Fe, New Mexico, and University of New Mexico Press, Albuquerque, New Mexico 1980.

Schaafsma, Polly, *Rock Art in New Mexico*, Museum of New Mexico Press, Santa Fe, New Mexico, 1992.

Schlanger, Sara H., "On Manos, Metates and The History of Site Occupations." *American Antiquity*, Vol. 56, pp. 460-474, July 1991.

Science News, "How To Date a Rock Artist." *Science News*, Vol., 139, p., 45, January 1991.

Setzler, P.M., "Seeking The Secrets of The Giants." *National Geographic*, Vol. CII, No.3, 1952.

Smith, Duane A., *Mesa Verde National Park—Shadows of the Centuries*, University Press of Kansas, Lawrence, Kansas, 1988.

Smith, Gary and Michael E. Long, "Utahs Rock Art—Wilderness Louvre." *National Geographic*, Vol. 157, No. 1, pp. 97-117, 1980.

Tanner, Clara Lee, *Prehistoric Southwestern Craft Arts*, University of Arizona Press, Tucson, Arizona 1976.

Turpin, Solveig A., "Rock Art and Hunter-Gather Archaeology:
A Case Study from Southwest Texas and Northern Mexico."
Journal of Field Archaeology, Vol. 17, pp. 263-281, 1990.

Tisdale, Shelby J., "From Rock Art to Wal-Mart: Kokopelli
Representations in Historical Perspective." *Archaeological
Society of New Mexico Papers*, Vol., 19, pp. 213-223. 1991.

Titiev, Mischa, "Story of Kokopelli." *American Anthropologist*,
Vol. 41, pp. 91-98, 1939.

Turner, Christy G., "Petroglyphs of the Glen Canyon Region."
Museum of Northern Arizona Bulletin 38, Glen Canyon Series,
No. 4, Flagstaff, Arizona, 1963.

Tyler, Hamilton, *Pueblo Animals and Myths*, University of
Oklahoma Press, Norman, Oklahoma, 1975.

Viola, Herman J., *After Columbus—The Smithsonian Chronicle of
North American Indians*, Smithsonian Books, Washington, D.C.
and Orion Books, New York, New York, 1990.

Walker, Steven L., *Indians of the American Southwest*
Camelback/Canyonlands Publishing, Flagstaff, Arizona, 1994.

Walker, Steven L., *The Southwest....A Pictorial History of the Land
and It's People*, Camelback/Canyonlands Publishing, Flagstaff,
Arizona, 1993.

Waters, Frank, *Book of the Hopi*, Viking Press, New York,
New York, 1963.

Wellman, K.F., "Kokopelli of Indian Paleology: Hunchbacked Rain
Priest, Hunting Magician, and Don Juan of the Old Southwest."

Journal of the American Medical Association,
Vol. 212, pp. 1678-1682, 1970.

Wellman, K.F., "Trends in North American Rock Art Research:
A Quantitative Evaluation of the Literature." *American
Antiquity*, Vol. XLV, No., 3, pp. 531-540, 1980.

Wright, Barton, "The Search for Kokopelli." *Arizona Highways*,
Vol. 69, pp. 14-17, 1993.

Young, John V., "Peregrinations of Kokopelli." *Westways (L.A.)*.
Vol. 57, No. 9, pp. 39-41, 1965.

Young, John V., *Kokopelli: Casanova of the Cliff Dwellers*, Filter
Press, Palmer Lake, Colorado, 1990.

Young, Mary Jane, *Signs From the Ancestors: Zuni Cultural
Symbolism and Perceptions of Rock Art*, University of New
Mexico Press, Albuquerque, New Mexico, 1988.

APPENDIX 2:
PRONUNCIATION GUIDE

Acoma	AH-koh-mah
Apache	ah-pah'chee
Chemehuevi	tchem-e-hway-vee
Cocopa	ko'ko-pah
Cochiti	KOH-chee-tee
Hano	ha'-NO
Havasupi	HAH-vah-soo-pie
Hohokam	HO-ho-KAHM
Hopi	Hoe'pee

FIRST MESA

Walpi	WAHL-pee
Sichomovi	si-cho'mo-vee
Hano	HAH-noh

SECOND MESA

Shungopovi	shung-OH-poh-vee
Mishongnovi	mee-SHONG-noh-vee
Shipaulovi	shi-paw'-lo-vee

THIRD MESA

Oraibi	oh-RAI-bee
Kiakochomovi	kee-ah-ko'-chom-o-vee
Hotevilla	hote'-vil-la

	Bakabi	bah'-ka-bee
	Moenkopi	mu'-en'ko'pee
Hualapai	wah'-lah-pie
Isleta	ees-LAY-tah
Jemez	hay'-mess
Jicarilla	Heek-ah-Reel-yah (Apache)
Katsina	cot-SEE-nah, also kachina, katchina and Kacina
Keres	Kay-rays
Kiva	KEE-vah
Laguna	lah-GOO-nah
Maricopa	mah-ree-ko'pah
Mescalero	mess-kah-lair-o (Apache)
Mogollan	MUGGY-own
Mohave	moh-hah-vee
Nambe	nahm-BAY
Navajo	na-vah-ho
Paiute	pie'-yoot
Picuris	pee-kuhr-EES
Pima	pee-mah
Pojoaque	poh-hwa-key
San Carlos	san CAR-los
San Felipe	san-faylee'pay
San Ildefonso	sahn-eel-day-FOHN-so
San Juan	san-HUAhn
Sandia	Sahn-dee'-yah
Santa Ana	Sahn-Ta-an-a
Santa Clara	SAHN-ta KLAH-rah

Santo Domingo	SAHN-toh doh-MEEN-go
Sichomoui	Si'-Cho'-MO-VEE
Taos	TAH-os
Tesuque	tay-SOO-kay
Tewa	TAY-wah
Tiwa	Tee-wah
Towa	TOH-wah
Tohono O'otam	to-ho'no o'-o-tam
(Known as Papago—pa-pa-go)	
Ute	yoot
Walpi	Wal-PEE
Yaqui	YAH-key
Yavapai	yah'vah'pie
Yuma	you-mah
Zia	Tsee'-ah
Zuni	zoo'-nee

APPENDIX 3:
GLOSSARY

Agave

(Ah-GA-Vee) are succulent relatives of lilies. The largest of these plants are called century plants or Mescal (Mess-Kahl) and the smaller ones are called Lechuguillas (Letch-You-hee Ahs). Three different drinks are made from the sap; Mescal (Mess-Kahl), Pulque (Pool-Kay) and Tequila (Tay-Keel-Ah). Fibers can be used to make Sisal. The young flower stalks and the heart of the leaf, Rosette, were used as food by the Indians in the Southwest. They also were a source for emergency water. Soap was made from the pulverized stems.

Amaranth

The seeds of the Amaranth plant are ground to make a flour. Amaranth flour is higher in protein than most other grains, and it is said to have more fiber than wheat and rice. It's believed to have started in this hemisphere in central tropical America. It is also said to be related to pigweed and tumbleweed.

ANCIENT MYTH & MODERN ICON

Anemia

A condition in which the amount of hemoglobin in the blood is low, causing the bloods oxygen carrying ability to be diminished. People experiencing anemia may feel weak, tired, faint or out of breath.

Anthropology

There are two types of anthropology, one is physical anthropology which is the study of man as a biological species, his past evolution and his physical characteristics. The other form of anthropology is social anthropology, which deals with social relationships, their significance and consequences, primarily in more primitive cultures and societies.

Archaeology

The study of the past through identification and interpretation of material remains of previous human cultures.

Archaic Period

A time in the Southwest when the foraging people the archeologists refer to as the Archaic, started occupying territories abandoned by the hunting people. This period occurred around 6,000 B.C. The first group of the Archaic have been referred to as the Cochise people. (see Cochise people).

Arthritis	The pain and suffering of joints. Arthritis can cause pain and limit the movements of the body. It is believed that previous trauma to the body can predispose bacterial infection, then lead to a more permanent condition like rheumatoid arthritis.
Astronomy	Considered the earliest of the sciences. Astronomy is in essence the study of the heavens. The study has been said to have been born at the crossroads of agriculture and religion.
Athabascan	Linguists designated these people as the Nadene. This includes the sub-family names of Tlingit, Eyak, Haida and Athabascan. They originally lived in an area that covered much of Alaska and large parts of northwestern Canada. Part of the Athabascans migrated to the Southwest and called themselves the Dine'e' which means "the people". They once again divided themselves into groups. We today refer to them as the Navajo, Apache and the Kiowa people.
Atlatl	Also known as a spear thrower, it was man's first efficient hunting tool. Its use began well before 1,000 B.C. and was used until replaced by bow and arrows between the time of Christ and 500 A.D. It was said to be about four feet

in length and was widely used by the Indians of the Southwest. The name, Atlatl, is said to come from the Aztec language word Nahuatle. It was probably developed as far back as 10,000 to 12,000 years ago.

Cacao   A tropical evergreen tree which bears a reddish-brown seed used to make chocolate.

Caliche   (Ca-Lee-Chee) is a soil with high concentrations of calcium carbonate and other mineral salts which creates a cement like consistency. The Hohokam culture used this in their building endeavors with many of their structures still standing today.

Caravel   A caravel is a sailing ship with lateen (fore-and-aft) sails. Columbus' ships, the Pinta and Nina were caravels.

Cholla Cactus   (Choh-Yahs) Are a plentiful sight in the southwestern Arizona desert. The three best known cholla are; Chainfruit Cholla, Teddybear Cholla and the Christmas Cholla. The cholla had multiple uses for the Indians of the Southwest. Its fruits and wood were used extensively in pre-modern times.

Clan

A formalized lineage, or family, group. Clans are usually named after animals or items found in their environment. Clans are family members of a common ancestor.

Cochise Culture

This culture was said to derive its name by scientists who named it for an ancient lake called Cochise which is now a dry desert basin called Willcox Playa in or around Cochise County in southwestern Arizona. The name is a base for subsequent cultural development among the various native American cultures in the Southwest. While the time span of this culture varies, it falls somewhere between 9000 and 6000 B.C.

Cremation

The ancient practice of reducing a corpse to its essential elements by burning. It is not known for sure how this practice began in the Southwest, but the Hohokam were cremating their dead before the time of Christ. It is interesting to note that the Greeks practiced cremation by as early as 1000 B.C.

Creosote	(Cree-Oh-Soat) Is an evergreen shrub of the desert Southwest. One of the oldest known living plants, radio carbon testing has found some to exceed 9,000 years of age. Mexicans refer to this bush as hediondilla which means "little stinker." The Indians used the creosote sap for mending pottery, waterproofing baskets, on arrow points and medicine. Teas were made from the branches and leaves to cure colds, intestinal problems, stomach and menstrual cramps. Modern scientists believe it may have value in dissolving kidney stones, and for painkillers. Its properties are also being looked at for anti-aging effects and control of cancer cells.
Dendrochronology	The study and dating of past events by the study of tree rings. The rings on trees create definite patterns, the rings differ based on amounts of moisture and sunlight that they receive annually. The rings and the ability to analyze them remain even when the wood becomes charcoal.
Ethnology	The scientific discipline dealing with the differing races of man, where he originated, man's distribution about the world, man's characteristics and the relationships between them. This is a form of anthropological study.

Ithyphallic	Erect penis.
Kachinas	Believed to be more than 500 different ancestral spirits who act as intermediaries between man and gods. Kachinas are supernatural beings associated with Pueblo origin myths. Kachinas are key to many of the Pueblo Indians religious practices. By using the kachinas masks and costumes, the Pueblo people feel that they can evoke the power of these beings. Kachinas are a primary source of communication between man and the gods.
Kivas	The word kiva is said to be a Hopi word. Kivas are subterranean circular rooms that primarily are used for ceremony and religious purposes, but are sometimes used as recreation, story telling, teaching and meeting places. The kiva was said to have originated from the pit houses used for living quarters by earlier generations. (see pit houses).
Legend	A story handed down from one generation to another which is believed but unverifiable to content. Most people view a legend and myth to be the same. (see mythology and lore).

Lore	Considered a traditional fact or belief. It's also defined as knowledge gained through experience and/or education. May or may not be verifiable in content. (See legend and mythology).
Mesoamerica	A somewhat generic name given to Mexico, Central and South America by writers. Prehistoric Meso America was a term used to describe the areas of Mexico from north of Mexico City to the south into Guatemala, Belize and into Honduras.
Metate	(meh-TAH-teh) The metate is one of the oldest known kitchen utensils in the Americas. It is similar to the molcajete (mohl-kahHEH-teh), but larger and rectangular in shape. Corn and/or other grains and chiles were ground with a rolling pin shaped stone that some refer to as Mano (MAH-noh) which means "hand" that is rolled back and forth over the material to be ground.
Millennium	1,000 years

Mythology	Traditional stories of a people which collectively communicate their folk history and that of their gods or heroes to provide affirmation of their culture. Myths provide rationalization for the mysteries within a culture by providing explanation to things unknowable. (see legend and lore).
Obsidian	A glass like rock used in arrow and spear points. The rock is usually black and is believed to be of volcanic origin. It is highly prized by Native Americans and collectors.
Osteoporosis	A bone disorder characterized by a reduction in bone density. Osteoporosis usually is accompanied by an increase in bone brittleness.
Petroglyphs	Images and designs created by pecking, chiseling, drilling or scratching dark desert rock surfaces to expose the lighter rock underneath. (From the Greek Petros, "rock", and Glyphe, "carving").
Phallic	Resembling of the phallus.
Phallism	Worship of the generative principle as symbol ized by the phallus.

Phallus

Symbol or representation of the penis.

Pictographs

Organic pigments and mineral pigments are made into paint and put on rocks in the form of images. (From the Latin Pictor, "painter", and the Greek, Graphein, "to write").

Piki Bread

Blue corn is traditionally used to make Piki. Piki bread is a kind of corn bread. Basically blue corn, water and a pinch of ashes are mixed into a thin gruel. The mixture is then spread on a smooth hot rock that rests above a fire. In a very short time, the mixture turns into what looks like wet parchment paper. At this point, it's peeled off and folded. Actually, several layers can be rolled together and this becomes very crisp when cooled. Some Piki, which is made by the same process but stuffed, looks like a Mexican tamale.

Pit Houses

Many believe that pit houses started as food pits or storage areas called cysts. Later they became subterranean living quarters when enlarged. The pit houses are also believed to be the forerunner of the kiva as the people started building their pueblo-style homes. (see kiva).

Priapism   A persistent and painful erection of the penis.
                       The causes are generally classified as nervous
                       or mechanical disorders. Spinal nerves can
                       cause this disorder. It has been associated with
                       tuberculosis.

Pochteca   Aztec and Toltec traders who traveled in
                       Mesoamerica. Some believe that they may have
                       come north to trade with the cultures of the
                       Southwest. It's said that they carried their wares
                       on their back and played a flute to announce
                       their arrival into the villages along the way.

Rorschach Test   Developed by Hermann Rorschach in 1920. It
                       is a test in which the subject describes what he
                       sees in a series of ten symmetrical inkblots. It's
                       believed that the interpretation of what a per-
                       son sees in those inkblots will reveal aspects of
                       their personality.

Saguaro   (Sah-War-Oh) is the largest of all U.S. cactus.
                       They have been known to grow up to 50 feet
                       tall and to reach ages of up to 200 years.
                       Saguaro fruits and wood were used extensively
                       by the indians of the Sonoran Desert. The
                       Tohono O'odham (Papago) and Pima Indians
                       still harvest the fruit which they eat raw and
                       the use the juice to make a wine

Shaman

(Sha'-Man) Shaman and medicine man are one and the same in most Native American cultures. Shamans were considered individuals of great power. Shamans are said to have the ability to mentally transport themselves through various levels of consciousness to communicate with the supernatural by means of trances, dreams, visions and fasting. Shaman are said to possess inborn sensitivities and to have sacred knowledge into healing. They have the ability to communicate with the spirit world. Their ability to travel beyond ordinary and traditional boundaries by altered states of awareness can allow them to see the future and travel not only great distances, but inward for knowledge of the human body and mind. Horns worn as a headdress are almost always emblematic of shamanistic and supernatural power. Birds may also symbolize the shaman power and magic of flight.

Sonoran Desert

The Sonoran Desert covers approximately 120,000 square miles. It covers southwestern Arizona, Southeastern California, most of the Mexican state of Baja, and the western half of the Mexican state of Sonora. The modern day tribes of the Papago and Pima call the Sonoran Desert home.

Stratigraphy

Known as a tool for archeological research, it basically is the study of strata (as in layers of clouds, rocks, soil or debris). The study advances the theory that most people would not dig down into a garbage pile to throw something away, so the items on top are the most recent to be used.

Tarahumara Indian

Also called Raramui Indians. They are said to be culturally related to the Yaqui and Mayo Indians, although they show similarities to the Pima-Papago cultures of the desert Southwest. They are small scale farmers who also keep a number of goats and cattle. They mostly reside in the northern Mexican state of Chihuahua.

Tuberculosis

Also known as TB, it is a disease caused by several species of mycobacterium, which collectively are referred to as the tubercle bacillus. While some forms of this disease affect the lungs, other forms affect bone and joints (as referred to the Kokopelli). It is said that this disease can spread in environments of poor hygienic standards and crowded conditions.

Yucca

Shrubs to small trees with evergreen dagger-like leaves. Yuccas are often confused with the agave, but agave blooms only once, while the yucca blooms each spring. There are 15 different yucca species. For early southwestern cultures the yucca provided food, fiber and building materials. The Native Americans used the yucca fibers to make cloth, sandals, baskets and matting material. As a food, they ate the buds and flower stalks as a vegetable. The roots were used to make soap.